VOTES FOR WOMEN

THE EVENTS ON MERSEYSIDE 1870 - 1928

Marij van Helmond

NATIONAL MUSEUMS & GALLERIES
• ON MERSEYSIDE •

British Library Cataloguing in Publication Data
Van Helmond, Marij
Votes for Women : Events on Merseyside, 1870-1928
I. Title
324.609427508
ISBN 0-906367-45-x
© Board of Trustees of the National Museums & Galleries on Merseyside
First Published in Great Britain 1992

CONTENTS

LIST OF ILLUSTRATIONS

ACKNOWLEDGEMENTS

I would like to thank everybody who has assisted with the exhibition *'Votes for Women - The Liverpool Story'*, which was held in the Museum of Labour History in 1989/1990 and which became the basis for this booklet; the individuals who lent the Museum their treasured objects or shared information about the topic; Mrs. S. Beeby, Miss Lois Bulley, Miss Irene Bullock, Ruth and Edmund Frow, Dr. J.K. Hulme, Miss A. James, Mr. H. Stevenson, Antonia Raeburn and Barbara Taylor.

Thanks also to Janet Smith, the archivist and the staff of the microfilm and reprographic units of Liverpool City Library, Adrian Allan, assistant archivist Liverpool University, David Doughan, Librarian of the Fawcett Library, and staff of the Southport and Wirral Public Libraries. My thanks to Edith Hamilton and Pat Ayers for their help and advice during the research period and their valuable comments on the drafts.

The illustrations are reproduced courtesy of the following:
British Library; 14, 19, 26, 32.
Documentary Photography Archive, Manchester; 34.
Fawcett Library, London; 30, 38.
Mrs. P. Francomb; 12, 37.
Miss A. James; 23, 29.
Lancashire Record Office, Preston; 13 (DDX 1137/3/87), 15 (DDX 1137/5/45), 24 (DDX 1137/5/46).
Liverpool City Record Office; 5,10.
Liverpool University Archives; 31.
Manchester Central Library; 4.
Museum of London; 18, 26.
National Council of Women, London; 6.
The Pankhurst Trust, Manchester; 9.
Antonia Raeburn; 17.
Mrs. M. Simey; 40.
Mr. H. Stevenson; 27, 28.
All other illustrations by the National Museums and Galleries on Merseyside.

FOREWORD

Exhibitions, however fascinating, tend to come and go leaving little wrack behind. Here we have a splendid exception to the rule. The organisers of the recent exhibition on Women's Suffrage in Liverpool are to be congratulated on having produced this admirable account of the material they tracked down in the course of assembling the exhibition. In so doing, they have rescued from oblivion a story of commitment and courage on the part of women in Liverpool which has never before received the tribute it deserves.

For me, reading this script is a happy indulgence in nostalgia. I knew so many of the women as living people. I was myself apprenticed to the great Eleanor Rathbone as a potential politician. I attended the celebratory dinner at the Bear's Paw when at last legislation was passed giving women like me the right to vote. I actually knew a real live suffragette who used to regale me with tales of how she had appeared in the Dale Street Courts, when I visited her second-hand bookshop just by the Cathedral. I even manage to make a (very minor) personal appearance in the last pages of the story.

Comparing then with now, there are differences galore and in my anecdotage I entertain the rising generation with tales of how we lived in those olden days. There's more to it than that, however. The position of women has changed beyond anything we ever dreamed of; at work, in marriage, in law, in status. But the difference that hits me with an almost physical impact is the lack of fire in the belly of the women's movement today.

The women whose activities are described in this book were inspired by their commitment to what they called *The Cause*. The right to vote was no mere political gimmick. It was the instrument by which they would achieve a much greater purpose. And that purpose was to set women free to take their place as responsible participating members of the society in which they lived.

Whatever has become of that blazing passion? The loss of all sense of purpose was symbolised for me in the latest County Council elections. The abolition of the six 'big Mets', of which Merseyside was one, meant that all those who lived in them were deprived of their right to vote on that occasion. And nobody seemed to care. Nobody marched the streets in protest, set fire to letter boxes, chained themselves to the gates of Downing Street. The women's movement of today, such as it is, has lost all sense of purpose. Women all too often opt out of their responsibilities as citizens.

The consequences are universally evident. The high rate of divorce. The phenomenon of the single parent. The dilemma of the incompatibility of career with marriage. The depreciation of the masculine role. These add up to as grievous a situation for women as anything they ever endured in those distant days of domestic bondage.

The lack of vision as to the way ahead leaves women all adrift in facing the unknown future which they now confront.

As Koestler put it, it is sometimes necessary to look back in order to go forward. The value of this record is that it enables women to set their current predicament in the context of the past. It will, I hope, serve to remind them of the richness of their heritage and in so doing, liberate them from the lack of vision which encumbers us today. The time is ripe for a new emancipation movement which will set women free from the dilemma in which they are trapped that they may be enabled to play their proper part in the century upon which we will shortly be entering.

Margaret Simey

INTRODUCTION

This booklet is an attempt to respond to requests received regularly by the Museum from school students, local history enthusiasts, women researching women's history or members of the public generally for information about 'the suffragettes' and whether they did anything in Liverpool.

It has been fairly simple to deal with the first question by offering a select reading list or by pointing in the direction of important collections of women's suffrage material elsewhere in the country. It has been difficult to say anything meaningful about women's suffrage activity locally because the information was not available.

Until recently the Museum itself held no material at all on the campaign and the little the Liverpool City Central Libraries possesses has no specific connection with Liverpool.[1] There seemed to be a general assumption that the issue of women's right to vote, which had led to so much activity in other towns and cities, had left Liverpool untouched.

Despite the fact that the literature on the women's suffrage movement in Britain could fill a room and that regularly fresh studies are being produced, there are actually very few concerned with the campaign as it took shape and was conducted on a local level. This was noted by Jill Liddington in her article *Rediscovering Suffrage History*[2] which introduces a study she and Jill Norris undertook on the role played by women textile workers in the movement in Lancashire, *One Hand Tied Behind Us*.[3] With the exception of their book there are only a handful of pamphlets and unpublished studies describing local campaigns.[4] There are several reasons for this.

One is that only recently the value of local studies for the understanding of national history has been appreciated. Charting of the activities and membership of local organisations helps to reveal the complexity of a national 'single issue' campaign such as the one for women's suffrage. For example, *One Hand Tied Behind Us* describes the contribution made by working class suffragists. At the same time, as a local case study, it allows a better understanding

Notes

1 The Picton Library of the Liverpool Central Library holds a box with a small collection of women's suffrage ephemera: a sash, some badges, photographs of national leaders and single issues of women's suffrage journals. It contains no Liverpool material. The Liverpool Record Office holds chapters in typescript and manuscript of Lady Constance Lytton's autobiographical *Prisons and Prisoners*.

2 J. Liddington, *Rediscovering Suffrage History,* History Workshop Journal, vol. 4, 1977, p. 192.

3 J. Liddington and J. Norris, *One Hand Tied Behind Us.* Virago, 1978.

4 E. King, *The Scottish Women's Suffrage Movement.* Glasgow, 1978. Gives information about local activities in Scotland. *Women in Wales, A documentary of Our Recent History,* Volume 1. Cardiff, 1987. Contains an illustrated article about the Swansea Suffragettes. Hexam New Opportunities for Women Course 1983-84. *Those Misguided Women. A Short History of the*

Campaign for Votes for Women in Tynedale. I. Dove, *Yours in the Cause. Suffragettes in Lewisham, Greenwich and Woolwich*. London, 1988.S.Peacock, *Votes for Women, The Women's Fight in Portsmouth*. Portsmouth Paper No. 39, 1983. C.E. Leech, *The Feminist Movement in Manchester, 1903-1914*. M A thesis, University of Manchester, 1971. About the movement in Manchester after the establishment of the WSPU. T. Berry, *The female suffrage movement in South Lancashire with particular reference to Oldham 1890-1914*. M A thesis Huddersfield Polytechnic, 1986. L. Leneman, *A Guid Cause. The Women's Suffrage Movement in Scotland*. Aberdeen, 1991. G.D. Heath, *The Woman's Suffrage Movement in and around Richmond and Twickenham*. Borough of Twickenham Local History Society, Paper No. 13, 1968.
5 B. Harrison, *Prudent Revolutionaries. Portraits of British feminists between the wars*. London, 1987.

of the connection between women's local economic position and the level of their political involvement.

Another reason is the scarcity of reliable sources for local studies. Whereas extensive collections of material have survived about the movement nationally, even for places where local activity was intense, such as Manchester, no significant body of evidence seems to have survived.

With regards to Liverpool or the wider area known as Merseyside, hardly any material is available. Perhaps this then explains the assumption that little activity took place here? If that assumption is correct, how can it be explained? Why should there have been activity in Manchester, Leeds, Salford, Rochdale, Preston and Wigan and not in Liverpool? If the assumption is wrong, then what was the nature of the campaign in Liverpool?

One of the few starting points for this investigation was Mary Stock's biography of Eleanor Rathbone, Liverpool's best known women's rights campaigner. It showed that Eleanor's involvement with the women's suffrage campaign had been considerable, but searches for primary sources associated with this have thrown up little of importance so far.[5] Material held in the Archives Department of the Manchester Central Library yielded some clues about early suffrage activity in Liverpool which could be followed up. A search of the national women's suffrage press proved fruitful and cross referencing of findings with reports in the local press resulted in a convincing picture of what must have been a truly lively women's suffrage 'scene' in Liverpool. Added to this has been information extracted from the national women's suffrage collections held in London and from contact with other researchers of the subject. When the writing up of this research was nearly completed, an unexpected primary source came to light in the form of diaries belonging to Dr. Alice Ker, Birkenhead G.P. and suffragist, which yielded some fresh data.

Merseyside women who suffered imprisonment for their support of "The Cause" and whose names are on the Roll of Honour of the WSPU.

Dorothy Abrahams
Alice Barton
Doris Callender
Helen Criddle
Bertha Elam
Georgina Healiss
Mrs Healiss
Amy Hetherington
Mrs Hillier
Mrs Hilton
Dr. Alice Ker
Margaret Ker
Bessie Morris
Alice Morrisey
Annie Myer
Constance Nugent
Mary C. Palethorpe
Gladys Roberts
Miss Taylor
Jessica Walker
Patricia Woodlock

Holloway prisoners, seated on the right Bertha Elam

1

BEFORE THE CAMPAIGN

It is outside the scope of this booklet to enter into the debate about the exact beginnings of the women's suffrage movement in Britain. Socio-political movements, such as the campaign for women's right to vote in national elections do not arise out of the blue and tend to have more than one cause. To establish whether it started in 1865 in London or in 1866 in London and Manchester simultaneously seems less important than trying to grasp what triggered it. Even that can be dealt with only very superficially here, but there are several excellent studies which offer a detailed analysis.[1]

Women's legal and social position in mid-Victorian times.
Women of the middle and upper classes were not expected to earn their own living but to be dependent on men; their fathers or their husbands. Under the law married women could not own property, whether inherited or, in rare cases, earned. The fact that some upper-class women were able to escape the law and have financial settlements drawn up before marrying does not diminish women's general economic dependence at that time.

Before 1857 it was almost impossible for women to obtain a divorce as this required a private Act of Parliament which could cost up to seven hundred pounds. Women could not have custody over their children. A father alone had legal rights over them and even after his death the mother would not be their legal guardian unless she had been made so in her husband's will.

Middle class women had little or no access to suitable paid work when they wanted or needed to earn their own living. They had no access to the medical or teaching professions or to the world of business. Nursing had not yet become a respectable area of paid employment and virtually the only acceptable kind of work was as a governess, a lowly paid job with very little status. Whereas working class women could, and increasingly were expected to work for themselves and their family, their pay was poor, conditions of work often appalling and ill health almost inevitably their lot.

Mrs Bulter at Liverpool, about 1866.

A major problem for women of all classes was the limited education they could expect to receive; working class girls received one or two years' primary education at the most, and middle and upper class girls received home tuition in socially acceptable subjects such as music, a language and some art.

Demand for change

Women's unequal status had been publicly criticised since the end of the eighteenth century by a few individual women and indeed men, but with very little impact.[2] Other brave women tried by means of practical actions to put right some of the many wrongs experienced by women. In Liverpool a small number of outstanding women made, in different ways, important contributions to improving the quality of Victorian women's lives.

In 1869, during the time she lived in Liverpool, **Josephine Butler**, wife of the Reverend George Butler, started her campaign against the Contagious Diseases Act of 1864. Under this Act women in ports like Liverpool could be forced by the police to undergo a medi-

Anne J. Clough

cal examination on the mere suspicion of prostitution. In her work with young destitute girls and women in Liverpool Josephine had been confronted with the suffering caused to women by this legislation. Through her campaign for

Notes

1 R. Strachey, *The Cause. A short history of the Women's Movement in Great Britain.* London, 1928. Reprint Virago 1978. Starts with women's legal and social position in society in 1792. S. Pankhurst, *The Suffragette Movement. An intimate account of persons and ideals.* London. 1931. Reprint Virago 1977. Devotes a chapter to the early days of the movement. R. Fulford, *Votes for Women, The Story of a Struggle.* London, 1958. With a chapter on the beginnings. C.Rover, *Women's Suffrage and Party Politics in Britain 1866-1914.* London, 1967. Concentrates on the political background of the campaign. T.Lloyd, *Suffragettes International. The world-wide campaign for women's rights.* London, 1971. A somewhat sweeping history with a

the repeal of the Act, which lasted fourteen years, Josephine challenged the attitudes of many Victorians towards women, sexuality and the family.[3]

Anne Jemima Clough was born in 1820 into a Liverpool middle class family. Unlike that of her brother Arthur, who went to Oxford University and became a well-known poet of his time, Anne's own education was very limited. This had made her painfully aware of the importance of educational opportunities for girls and women. She became involved with the movement for higher education for women outside universities. The campaign was successful and gained ground in many cities and towns. Anne became secretary of the North of England Council for the Promotion of Higher Education for Women. In 1870 she became the first Principal of Newnham, the first women's college connected with Cambridge University.[4]

Jeannie Mole grew up in London and came to Liverpool in 1879. Soon after, she married the prosperous Liverpool fruit merchant Keartland Mole and moved to the Wirral. As a socialist she

Jeannie Mole, Socialist and Women's Trade Union Worker.

was shocked by the poverty she encountered amongst working class women in Liverpool and made it her life's mission to help them to help themselves. She saw trade unions as the most effective way for women to fight for better conditions and took the initiative for the establishment of unions for women, a controversial step at the time.

Meanwhile, in 1865 a small band of London women began to meet regularly. They were mainly middle class, intelligent and unmarried and shared an interest in educational opportunities for women. They argued that women's lot would not improve until they could elect the people who made the laws which so affected their lives. At that time only men (although not *all* men) could vote in national elections and only men could stand as Parliamentary candidates. It seemed important that women could at least elect those men whom they knew would represent their interests in the House of Commons. They started to collect signatures for a petition which asked the Government to give women householders the right to vote on the same basis as men. This petition was presented to Parliament on their behalf by John Stuart Mill, M.P., in 1866. It was heavily defeated but the members of the action group were not. On the contrary, one of Britain's longest lasting campaigns was born! Groups similar to the one in London were rapidly established elsewhere and within the year Manchester, Edinburgh and Bristol had their own 'Women's Suffrage Societies'.

To combine the strength of local societies the 'National Union of Women's Suffrage Societies' (NUWSS) was set up. Its sole aim was to press the Government '*To Grant Women In Britain The Vote As It Is, Or May Be Accorded To Men*'. The Union was not connected with either the Tory or the Liberal Party (the Labour Party did not yet exist) and was committed to lawful and peaceful campaigning strategies.

chapter on the beginnings, useful for the international context.
2 M. Wollstonecraft, *A vindication of the rights of women.* 1792. Reprint Penguin. W. Thompson, *Appeal of one half of the human race.* London 1825. R.J. Richardson, *The Rights of Woman.* 1840. Reprint Working Class Movement Library, 1986. J.S. Mill, *On the subjection of Woman.* London, 1869.
3 J. Butler, *Personal Reminiscences of a Great Crusade.* London, 1898.
4 B.A. Clough, *A memoir of Anne Jemima Clough.* 1897.

2

THE EARLY DAYS, 1870 - 1907

To understand when and how the issue of women's right to vote took root in Liverpool, it helps to cast the net wider and look at the whole of Merseyside. This may seem odd as it is often argued that Merseyside, as a geographical concept, is of little use for the investigation of social and cultural phenomena. As a local authority it was created only recently for political reasons and the districts which together make up Merseyside are said to have little or nothing in common today, nor did they in the past.

Southport and St. Helens are really Lancashire, the Wirral is Cheshire and Liverpool, well, is Liverpool. However, if the sources used for an investigation into the local history of the women's suffrage campaign are reliable, a different picture emerges.

The first stirrings
The first issue of the first women's suffrage journal, published in March 1870 by that Manchester champion of 'The Cause', Lydia Becker, lists as members of the Manchester Society, five Liverpool residents. Two of the names have a special ring as they are those of Josephine Butler and her husband, the Reverend George Butler.[1] Also listed is Mr. Andrew Leighton, prominent member of the local Liberal Party. He spoke in 1869 at a public meeting on the newly won right for women to vote in *local* elections, and argued that this right should be extended to parliamentary elections. No other public meetings or activities are reported for Liverpool and it seems safe to conclude that Liverpool sympathisers with the campaign had to turn to Manchester for information and contacts.

In 1872, the *Women's Suffrage Journal* reports a Liverpool committee with the Butlers, Mr. Andrew Leighton and a Miss Pendlebury as members and a Mrs. McTaggart as Honorary Secretary. However small, this committee must have offered a link with activities elsewhere.

The *Women's Suffrage Journal* also mentions a Birkenhead Committee, with a Mrs. W. Binns, Oak Bank, Oxton Road

THE LATE MISS LYDIA BECKER.
(From a Photograph by Warwick Brookes.)

as President and Mrs. J.G. O'Brien, Fern Nook, Woodchurch Road as Honorary Secretary.

A year later the *Women's Suffrage Journal* briefly reports a conference of the Liverpool group of the National Society for Women's Suffrage, held in December 1872 in the Bible Society Rooms, Slater Street. The annual report (which seems to point in the direction of a well-established group) was read out and reported 'steady progress and good work done by the branch during the year'. Amongst this good work may well have been the organisation of a meeting in April 1873, in Hope Hall, Hope Street. The meeting, a public one, was about the question of women as voters in national politics and attracted a 'crowded assemblage'. According to the reporter of *The Porcupine*, Liverpool's satirical weekly, '...It was evident that the majority of persons were attracted more by curiosity than by sympathy'.[2] Whether he was right in this or not, clearly the issue of women's suffrage could pull a crowd in Liverpool. Lydia Becker, star-speaker of the evening, was received with a mixture of cheering and hissing, apparently because of criticism she had expressed in the past of the Christian religion and the little it had done for women.

The reporter's own ambivalence on the issue comes across as he grudgingly concedes that the lady-speakers did perhaps deserve the vote for 'their display of masculine intelligence' but that they had a higher vocation in life than becoming involved with sordid politics. 'To be the head of a happy home, the mother of a loving family, is women's best and highest mission. The woman who is compelled into the coarse career of masculine pursuits is an exile from her true home. She is carried off, as it were, a prisoner by savages'.[3]

In April 1873 the *Women's Suffrage Journal* reported an enthusiastic public meeting under the auspices of the Birkenhead Branch of the National Society for Women's Suffrage, presided

Hope Hall, now the Everyman Theatre, as it was in 1870.

Notes

1 *Manchester National Society for Women's Suffrage Journal* (W.S.J.), No. 1, 1.3.1870. The other members were Miss Eileen Bibby, and a Mrs. Lister from Seaforth.

2 *The Porcupine*, 5.4.1873, p.4.

3 ibid.

4 W.S.J., April 1880, p.26.

5 W.S.J., 1.11.1880, p.191. This meeting was also extensively reported in the Liverpool Daily Post and Mercury (LDP&M), 28.10.1880, p.6.

6 Women gained the right to vote in municipal (local) elections in 1869.

over by Mrs. Binns, wife of the Rev. W. Binns. A Mrs. Nosworthy eloquently addressed the meeting saying, amongst other things, that 'Two-and-a-half millions of women had to feed themselves without the aid of male support. Surely such as these had a right to be represented in Parliament; and it seemed to her that the denial of the franchise to those winners of bread, simply because they were females, was an arbitrary exercise of power.'

In 1880 the *Women's Suffrage Journal* mentions an 'At Home' held by Mrs. Thomas Brocklebank, wife of the influential Liverpool shipping merchant, at her residence, 72 Huskisson Street.[4] This meeting was 'numerously attended' and amongst those present were Mrs. R.D. Holt, wife of the President of the Liverpool Liberal Association, Mr. William Rathbone, Liberal M.P. and Lady Ramsay whose husband was standing as Liberal candidate for the parliamentary elections of that year. In the same year the *Women's Suffrage Journal* devoted a two-page article to another event: 'Women and the Municipal Contest, Meeting of Women at Hope Hall'.[5] There are two interesting points to note about this meeting. The first is that it aimed to interest women in the use of a right they had recently won; i.e. the right to vote in local (or municipal) elections,[6] and the second that this was a 'women only' public meeting! The meeting was opened with the reading of a letter from Josephine Butler, who was unable to attend because of illness. In it she stressed that women who could vote had a duty to do so and should elect local councillors sympathetic to women's rights. Such councillors could do much for women in municipal affairs and help to increase respect for women generally.

Lydia Becker, this time warmly received, spoke along much the same lines and pointed out that for example Manchester City Council had passed a resolution pledging support for Women's Suffrage in general elections. She advised women voters to sharply quiz the local candidates about their individual stance on women's suffrage before voting for them. At the end of the meeting a resolution was moved asking the Council of Liverpool to submit a petition to the House of Commons in favour of women's suffrage. The resolution was carried unanimously.

On the basis of the events described so far, however interesting, it is difficult to say whether they can be seen as an expression of a coherent local campaign. Apart from the public meetings mentioned, most activity seems to have taken place in the homes of a handful of middle and upper class women mainly connected with the local Liberal Party.

The Southport connection

There is evidence that the initiative towards a formal, permanent organisation in Liverpool was actually taken by Southport women. This course of events offers an interesting case study of how women tended to organise, through their personal social networks rather than through formal public structures.

During the 1870s Southport, like Liverpool, had experienced the public meetings attended by national speakers as well as a number of meetings in private homes. By 1888 there is evidence of an active organisation called the Southport Guild of Women's Household Suffrage. Judging by its name this Society supported a limited measure of women's suffrage, i.e. for women householders only which excluded married women from the claim. Although there was disagreement about such a stance within the movement at large, at least Southport boasted a formal women's suffrage society which held regular public meetings. Not content with this, the Southport women must have decided to cast their net wider, as transpires from an article in the *Southport Visiter*:

'If further evidence of the earnestness of purpose of the Southport Guild of the Unrepresented were wanted, its latest achievement would supply it. Under its auspices a public meeting to consider the subject of female Household Franchise was held last night in the Rotunda Hall, Liverpool and in spite of the night being one on which the fashionable Philharmonic concerts are given, and a wet cold evening to boot, sufficient interest was aroused by our indefatigable towns-women to cause an audience of not far short of a thousand people to assemble...'[7]

7 *Southport Visiter* (SV), 12.4.1888, p.6.
8 Letter 17.2.1893, Manchester Central Library, Archives Department, M50/2/1/194.

To the surprise of the *Southport Visiter* the resolutions about women's suffrage were carried with enthusiasm and at the close of the meeting the Southport Honorary Secretary, Mrs. Sherbrooke, was asked to form a branch of the Guild in Liverpool, '...a town which has hitherto shown little or no interest in the matter'. And with an approving nod in the direction of the Southport women: 'The difficulty of arousing interest and organising a meeting in a large town like Liverpool, and where the individual members of the Guild are quite unknown, would be enough to appal most men, but the fact that the difficulty was attacked, and most triumphantly overcome, shows that the Southport ladies not only have courage and energy, but religious belief in the justice of their cause and the urgency of the reform they advocate'. What the reporter of this meeting was not aware of was the way in which women's networks operated. The Southport women may not have been known to the Liverpool citizenry at large, but they had powerful personal connections in Liverpool and knew how to use them.

In the early days of the movement the setting up of a local branch was often the result of local leading ladies inviting national figures in the movement to give a public lecture or be a guest of honour at a drawing-room meeting. The local initiative-taker often already knew the national figure from other organisations or through family connections. In Liverpool's case for example, Mrs. Agnes Brocklebank, who thirteen years earlier had hosted an 'At Home' on women's suffrage for Liberal Party members, wrote to Mrs. Fawcett, the National Leader of the NUWSS.[8] There was to be a political rally in Liverpool opposing Irish Home Rule and Mrs. Fawcett, a known opponent of Home Rule, had been invited as a speaker. Mrs. Brocklebank wrote to her on the request of the local Liberal Party asking her *not* to use the meeting as a platform for women's suffrage. From the bantering tone of her letter it is safe to conclude that Mrs. Brocklebank knew Mrs. Fawcett informally.

Equally **Mrs. Allan Bright**, wife of a prosperous Liverpool lawyer and shipping merchant and leading Liberal, who lived at 10, Mill Bank, West Derby, recounted in an interview she gave in 1895 how she had been present at the meeting in the Rotunda, where the decision to set up a Liverpool branch had been taken. It was she, Mrs. Bright, who subsequently invited Mrs. Fawcett to the meeting at which the Liverpool Women's Suffrage Society (LWSS) was finally formed.[9] Mrs. Bright had been a member of the Southport Guild at whose meeting she had got to know Mrs. Fawcett...

the early women's suffrage movement in Liverpool. There was **Mrs. Alfred Booth**, an American woman who had married the wealthy Liverpool shipowner Alfred Booth and lived with her family at 46 Ullet Road. Like Mrs. Bright she was on the executive committee of the Liverpool Ladies Union of Workers Among Women and Girls, an organisation which counted a range of socially minded women in Liverpool amongst its members and which organised powerful national conventions on women's welfare.

Mrs Alfred Booth

Mrs Allan Bright

Mrs. Bright was one of a trio of Liverpool ladies who between them dominated the social and welfare work as well as

Nessie Muspratt on the day she became Mrs Egerton Stewart-Brown.

9 S.A.Tooley, Ladies of Liverpool, in *The Woman at Home*, 1895.
10 *Liverpool Courier* (LC), 10.4.1894.
11 *Annual Report of the Central Committee of the National Society for Women's Suffrage*, 1896.

The third lady was **Mrs. Egerton Stewart Brown**, née Nessie Muspratt, whose brother was Max Muspratt, Liberal politician and founder of ICI. She lived at 16, Ullet Road. She was President of the Liverpool Women's Liberal Association and active in a range of women's organisations. All three of them were on the first executive committee of the LWSS.

The first formal meeting of the LWSS took place in January 1894 and in April the *Liverpool Courier* reported that the LWSS was 'in thoroughly working order', and holding a meeting in the Temperance Hall in Hardman Street.[10] At the first Annual General Meeting on 11 January 1895 Mrs. Bright, now secretary of the LWSS, was able to report a satisfactory increase in members since the formation of the society.

The year before the Birkenhead Women's Suffrage Society had been established[11] with a Miss Mellor as secretary and in 1898 this branch changed its name to Birkenhead and Wirral Women's Suffrage Society. Thus by the end of the 1890s the whole of Merseyside had become fully organised and active around the issue of women's suffrage.

A Newcomer on the Scene
The Merseyside branches of the NUWSS followed closely the style and tactics of campaigning developed by the national organisation. One reason for this was the very existence of the network of women already mentioned. National and local leaders of the movement had regular contact with each other which promoted a unified approach to the campaign by local branches. Leaders and members tended to be from similar class backgrounds and political persuasion and the style of campaigning developed suited all of them, wherever they lived.

The NUWSS had stated from the very beginning that, although they were quite prepared to run a tough campaign, this would not involve any unlawful or unconstitutional activities. It was also their policy that the campaign was not to be tied to either political party, Conservative or Liberal, but aimed to persuade individual M.P.s to support the cause. This approach, non-party political and law abiding, made it possible to bring many women together in one umbrella organisation.

The chosen tactics of the NUWSS and its branches were to educate local women (and men) through public meetings and publicity material, to lobby politicians in Whitehall or at fashionable 'At Homes', to organise petitions and campaigns during election time. These tactics, used until the beginning of the new century did not produce a great deal of tangible results. Undoubtedly knowledge about the issue among the public had increased, and so had the number of women supporting the demand. The number of politicians from both parties sympathetic to the women had also increased but this support did not result in either party making women's right to vote into an election issue. Despite numerous debates in Parliament between 1866 and 1900 there was never enough support for any Women's Suffrage Bill to become an Act of Parliament.

In 1903 an event took place which led to a serious challenge to the NUWSS

and its kind of campaigning. The history of this has been extensively documented elsewhere and for an appreciation of its effect on Women's Suffrage in Liverpool it will be enough to recall a few facts.[12]

In Manchester Mrs. Emmeline Pankhurst, wife of a local lawyer with socialist sympathies, had been involved with the campaign almost from its beginnings. She had become thoroughly dissatisfied with the lack of success

Mrs Pankhurst's house at 62 Nelson Street, Manchester, has recently been restored and now houses a thriving women's centre.

12 S. Pankhurst, *The Suffrage Movement,* London 1931. Reprint London 1978. Detailed account of the start of the Women's Social and Political Union, based on personal recollections. A.Raeburn, *Militant Suffragettes.* London, 1973. A.Rosen,*Rise Up, Women, The Militant Campaign of the Women's Social and Political Union 1903-1914.* London, 1974. M.Mackenzie,*Shoulder to Shoulder.* London 1975. Of interest mainly for its illustrations.

which she saw as entirely due to the unwillingness of any politician of whatever party to take the women's demand seriously. She felt that a different way of campaigning was now required and in 1903 she called a meeting of local women in her house in 62 Nelson Street at which a new suffrage organisation, the Women's Social and Political Union (WSPU) was established.

Even the name of the new organisation reflected its determination to be different: women could and should be politically aware and active if they were to win equal rights with men. Initially the WSPU remained small until in October 1905 developments took a dramatic turn. Mrs. Pankhurst's daughter Christabel and her friend Annie Kenney managed to get themselves arrested and gaoled, having heckled Sir Edward Grey who spoke as Liberal candidate at an election meeting in the Free Trade Hall in Manchester. The incident hit the headlines of local and national newspapers and overnight the issue of women's suffrage became what its campaigners had wanted it to be all the time: *NEWS*.

It changed the nature of the fledgeling organisation. The action of the young women and the willingness of the WSPU to defend it appealed to women in Britain in an unexpected way. The membership of the WSPU expanded, its headquarters were moved from Manchester to London and the Pankhursts and their friends became its leaders and national figures. The WSPU employed organisational methods different from those of the NUWSS, more 'modern' almost. The informal women's network remained an important force but the organisation also employed women as paid local organisers and used shop-front premises as well as private drawing rooms for contact with the public. A very sophisticated publicity machinery was developed as the WSPU grasped the importance of using what are now called 'the media'.

The early WSPU in Liverpool
The WSPU did not develop proper branches until after it had moved to London although its Manchester members travelled the North West widely, speaking at every possible event or occasion on the question of women's

suffrage. There is evidence that Adela Pankhurst, Mrs. Pankhurst's youngest daughter, spoke in Liverpool before 1906.

On 9 January 1906 the Prime Minister, Sir Henry Campbell Bannerman, spoke at a large rally of Liberals in the Sun Hall, Kensington. His lengthy speech, (mainly dealing with the issue of Free Trade), was interrupted on a number of occasions by women in the audience who jumped up, waving banners shouting: 'Will you vote for women's suffrage?' and 'Will the Liberal Government give working women the vote?' The newspaper reports give no indication who these women were but Mrs. Pankhurst in her memoirs mentions this meeting: '...at Sun Hall, Liverpool, addressed by the Prime Minister, nine women in succession asked the important question and were thrown out of the Hall; this in the face of the fact that Sir Campbell Bannerman was an avowed suffragist.'[13] A letter to the Editor in the *Liverpool Daily Post and Mercury* of 12 January 1906 signed by Eleanor Rathbone explains that the disturbance had not been caused by members of the LWSS.

In fact they had found the event distasteful and unnecessary because the Prime Minister was known to be a supporter. It seems safe to assume that the women in the meeting were WSPU members mainly from outside Liverpool. All this caused great excitement amongst women on Merseyside and the pros and cons of this sort of 'militant' and unfeminine behaviour were hotly debated. At a meeting of the Wallasey Socialist Society in Liscard Hall Mrs. Pankhurst was one of the speakers in defence. She said that, since

The Liberal Rally at the Sun Hall

SCENE AT THE SUN HALL.

13 E.Pankhurst, *My Own Story*. London, 1914, p.52. Reported also in *LDP&M*, 10.1.1906, p.7. See also S.Pankhurst, *The Suffragette Movement*, p.195.

14 *Wallasey News* (WN), 13.1.1906, p.2.

15 *ibid*, 11.1.1906.

16 A Liverpool branch of the Fabian Society was established in 1892 and was a flourishing organisation until the First World War. It counted most of Liverpool's Socialists amongst its members and its women members were particularly active.

17 H.Mitchell, *The Hard Way Up*, 1968. Reprint Virago 1977, p.142-149. The incident was also extensively reported in the *Labour Record*, June-July, 1906.

18 *Suffragette*, 22.11.1912.

women didn't come within the pale of the law, they could go outside it and use revolutionary methods. The best way to end all this, was to make women citizens![14] But the *Wallasey News* in its 'Ladies Column' stated that the misbehavers could rightly be called 'political viragos'.[15]

In June of the same year a women's suffrage meeting took place in the Temperance Hall in Hardman Street, presided over by the radical Canon Kempthorne. One of the Misses Pankhurst spoke with 'remarkable eloquence' and Mrs. Bright of the LWSS told the audience how she took part in a delegation to lobby the Prime Minister and how he had yawned through the meeting with them. Clearly even within the LWSS mixed feelings were beginning to creep in about some Government members' attitudes towards the issue.

At that time one Liverpool woman is known to have been particularly active in the Manchester WSPU. Alice Morrissey was the wife of Liverpool's first socialist councillor and an active Fabian in her own right.[16] She was a friend of Hannah Mitchell, a member of the Manchester Independent Labour Party (ILP), who in turn was friendly with the Pankhursts; women's networks again! In June 1906 Alice Morrissey, Adela Pankhurst and Hannah Mitchell were amongst a large crowd attending a Liberal Rally at Belle Vue, Manchester. They and seven other women were thrown out of the Hall for heckling the speaker. When Alice's husband who was with them protested, he was also dragged out and the four were arrested and charged at the police station. A week later they were all up in court charged with obstruction and Adela and Hannah with assault of a policeman![17] When given the choice between a fine or imprisonment the women chose the latter. The fine for Alice's husband was soon paid by friends concerned about his health and he was released the next day. Alice remained in Strangeway Prison until the week after. Once a Liverpool WSPU branch was established she became very active in it and remained so until her untimely death in 1912.[18] The first time such a branch is officially mentioned is in the first issue of the WSPU's own newspaper, *Votes for Women*, in October 1907.

3

SAME AIM, DIFFERENT TACTICS, 1907-1912

In 1907 Liverpool, and most other parts of Merseyside, boasted local branches of the two most important national organisations for women's suffrage. Between them they generated a great deal of activity which involved large numbers of local women. Hardly a week passed by between 1907 and 1914 without the movement being mentioned in the local press, favourably or unfavourably. Before giving an account of some of their activities it seems worthwhile briefly to consider who the active local women were and what motivated them. Since no personal accounts of local activities have survived (with the exception of a fragment of a taped interview and some diary notes),[1] our main source of information is the local newspapers and the women's suffrage press itself. For several years both the NUWSS and the WSPU published weekly national papers in which there are regular reports on activities and events 'in the provinces.' These make it possible to check with the local papers details of the events, to find names of the women involved and to get an impression (but no more than that) of how they experienced what was happening.

The Liverpool Women's Suffrage Society
Since 1897 the LWSS had been headed by **Eleanor Rathbone** as the Honorary Secretary of its Executive Committee. Then twenty five years old she lived with her parents in Greenbank and was heavily involved with local, social and welfare affairs rather than with national issues which she adopted later on. Her politics were 'independent' in that she held no formal party membership but by upbringing and temperament she was a progressive Liberal. With her interest in the lot of women generally it was inevitable that she should have become involved in the struggle for the vote.[2]

GRANBY WARD
MUNICIPAL ELECTION, November 1st, 1910.

Miss ELEANOR RATHBONE,
THE INDEPENDENT CANDIDATE,

Supported by the following among others:

ALDERMAN SIR WILLIAM BOWRING, BART., J.P.
SIR B. S. JOHNSON, J.P.
DR. BICKERTON.
BURTON W. ELLIS, ESQ., C.C.
ALEXANDER GUTHRIE, ESQ.
REV. CANON HARFORD.
A. E. JACOB, ESQ., C.C.
JOHN JAPP, ESQ., J.P., C.C.
T. HARRISON JONES, ESQ., J.P., C.C.
HUGH JONES, ESQ.
WILLIAM JONES, ESQ., P.L.G.
JOHN LEA, ESQ., J.P., C.C.

REV. H. H. MATTHEW,
JOHN MORRIS, ESQ., J.P., C.C.
A. LYLE RATHBONE, ESQ., C.C.
H. R. RATHBONE, ESQ., C.C.
W. B. STODDART, ESQ., J.P.
W. E. WOODHALL, ESQ.
MRS. EGERTON STEWART-BROWN.
MISS F. L. CALDER.
MISS GEORGIANA CROSFIELD, P.L.G.
DR. MARY BURRELL DAVIES.
MRS. ELLIS, P.L.G.
MISS E. C. GREENE.
MISS FLORENCE MELLY.

Committee Room: 85, Granby Street. Open 10 a.m. to 9-30 p.m.

Hon. Secretary of Miss Eleanor Rathbone's Election Committee:
Miss OLIVE JAPP, 9, Alexandra Drive.

Notes
1 Interview with Bertha Clare, a Liverpool suffragette, by Barbara Taylor, BBC Radio Merseyside, 1968.
2 M. Stocks, *Eleanor Rathbone, A Biography.* London, 1949.

The other members of the Liverpool executive committee were local leading ladies with backgrounds similar to those of Eleanor – families of merchants, bankers and lawyers, Liberal in politics and often connected with the Unitarian Church. The older women such as Mrs. Bright, Mrs. Booth and Mrs. Stewart-Brown had been involved with the campaign since the 1880s. The younger ones had become involved through personal acquaintance with Eleanor or through work for the good causes she supported. The same names keep cropping up during the period of development of the LWSS from 1900 until 1914 and after the War until 1928.

Jane Colquitt, on the left, touring the Lancashire villages to raise support for 'The Cause'.

Miss Wyse became secretary of the Birkenhead WSS in 1900 but was also active in the Liverpool branch, for example during the 1910 election campaigns. Other activists were Miss Meade-King (daughter of the Liberal Councillor, later Alderman, R. Meade-King), Jessie Beavan (sister of Liverpool's first woman Lord Mayor Margaret Beavan), Evelyn Deakin, Cicely Leadly-Brown and Edith Eskrigge. The latter became a paid organiser for the West Lancashire, West Cheshire and North Wales Federation of Women's Suffrage Societies and established new branches throughout the region.[3] Jane Colquitt, daughter of a Liverpool captain-pilot, was invited to become involved after she accidentally had attended a national conference of the NUWSS in London.

A notable exception to this pattern of local, predominantly upper and middle class Liberalism was Doctor Alice Ker. Having initially been very active in the Birkenhead branch of the NUWSS she 'crossed over' to the WSPU in 1909 and remained active in the Liverpool branch until 1914.[4] It seems relevant to mention also the connection between

Eleanor Rathbone and the working class suffragist from Nelson, Selina Cooper.[5] In the early days Selina had campaigned for women's suffrage alongside Mrs. Pankhurst, as both were also members of the Independent Labour Party. However, she left the WSPU feeling that it was not sufficiently sensitive to the plight of working class women. She became an organiser for the NUWSS and in that capacity worked in Liverpool on several occasions during election time. Eleanor, who saw the value of having somebody like Selina in Liverpool, used her to get working class women interested in women's suffrage. When in Liverpool Selina would stay in Eleanor's house in Greenbank and the two women maintained contact throughout their lives.

Education

In line with the NUWSS the LWSS saw education as one of its main tasks. Its supporters knew that the arguments for women having the right to vote were not so widely understood as they might have wished. They also knew that many women, both working and middle class, had themselves strong reservations about it albeit for different reasons.

3 The West Lancashire, West Cheshire and North Wales Federation was formed in 1911 to bring together all the local branches of the National Union of Women's Societies in the area. An organiser was appointed to establish new branches and co-ordinate fund-raising and publicity.
4 See Chapter 5.
5 J. Liddington, *The Life and Times of a Respectable Rebel. Selina Cooper 1864-1946*. London, 1984.

LIVERPOOL WOMEN'S SUFFRAGE SOCIETY.

Greenbank,
Liverpool, E.

5th March, 1907.

Dear Sir,

The Committee of the above Society believe that there are many organisations of working men, who, at this time when the question of Women's Suffrage is so prominently before the country, would be glad of an opportunity of hearing the case stated from the woman's point of view. They would therfore be very glad to arrange for their organiser, Mrs Cooper, or for one of their members, to address your Society on any evening that could be mutually arranged if possible within the next fortnight.

Mrs Cooper, now a Poor-Law Guardian of Nelson, was a worker in a cotton mill before marriage; she is an excellent speaker and could, I think, tell you much that would interest your members as to the view taken of this question by the skilled and organised women workers in the textile industries.

I am, Sir,

Yours faithfully,

Elen I. Rathbone

Hon. Secretary.

Mr I. Newton,
   Amalgamated Society of Carpenters and Joiners.

Middle and upper class Victorian women brought up with the notion that the world of politics was a man's world thought it unfeminine to want to take part in it. Moreover, upper class women could exercise considerable political influence anyway through their menfolk if they wanted to.

Working class women did not see fighting for the right to vote as unfeminine but as irrelevant; they could not see what there was in it for them. If the vote was going to be given to women on the same basis as to men, i.e. to householders with a certain annual income, how many working class women would benefit? In any case, how could voting rights make a difference to exploitation at work, poverty and ill health?

Eleanor Rathbone and her campaigners made it their business to deal with these reservations – pointing out that in fact it was women's duty to get involved with politics if they wanted a better world for themselves and their children. The LWSS did not omit to address men as well, trying to convince them that it was in their interest to support women in their demand.

Lobbying and Petitions

The LWSS made much use of the contact its leaders had with leading members of the Liberal Party to whom they were either related or in whose circles they moved. Through them they received information about what was actually going on in Parliament, and what the mood was of the Prime Minister of the day and his Cabinet Ministers. Through them they were able, or so they thought, to influence Parliamentary proceedings by putting pressure on individual M.P.s to vote in a particular way. Eleanor Rathbone, once she had been elected a local councillor in 1909, lost no time in moving a resolution at one of the first council meetings she attended. In this the Council was asked to add to the pressure on the Government in favour of women's suffrage. Her resolution was passed with 44 votes to 20 – the first time the Liverpool Council formally came out in support of women's voting rights.[6]

The LWSS also used canvassing as a way of bringing the issue to the attention of people. It used the result of such canvasses as further ammunition especially in its debate with the anti-suffrage organisation which argued that there was no really significant support in Liverpool for women's voting rights.[7]

Social Events and Demonstrations

It seems that the LWSS preferred a programme of regular, small scale events to mass meetings and demonstrations. It would hire a small, popular venue, such as the Yamen Cafe in Bold Street, and organise an evening with a well known speaker as main attraction. Local members would jolly up these events with poetry reading, singing or a performance by the Blue Bird Theatre Company, a group of four Liverpool women offering acting and ballet. On occasion, though, the LWSS would take part in larger events and two of these spring to mind.

In June 1908 the NUWSS organised its first mass demonstration in London's Hyde Park. Members of all the Merseyside branches travelled to London on a specially hired train to take part in this demonstration. The event was extensively covered by the local newspapers and even photographs were taken of the departure of the Merseyside contingent from Central

6 *Liverpool City Council Minutes,*1.2.1911. Liverpool Record Office.
7 See Chapter 6, The Anti Women's Suffrage Society.
8 *Liverpool Football Echo,* 13.6.1908, p.3.

Liverpool Suffragists boarding the London train at Central Station.

SUNDAY, JUNE 15, 1908.

Women's Suffrage

HUGE DEMONSTRATION IN LONDON.

GREAT MARCH AND MEETING.

STRIKING SPECTACLE.

10,000 ENTHUSIASTS.

WITH THE LIVERPOOL CONTINGENT.

(BY OUR SPECIAL LADY CONTRIBUTOR.)

The National Union of Women Suffrage Societies made a magnificent effort on Saturday to convince the Prime Minister that a great number of women were in earnest in their demand for the abolition of the sex qualification in the matter of Parliamentary

Station and of them marching behind a Liverpool banner on the Embankment in London.[8]

On the evening of June 18, 1910 a 'monster demonstration' took place outside St. George's Hall organised by a range of Liverpool organisations supporting women's suffrage. It was intended in support of yet another Private Member's Bill for women's suffrage coming before Parliament. There were three platforms on St. George's Plateau from which speakers addressed the crowd simultaneously. (No Public Address systems in those days!). There was a glittering range of speakers representing all the groups involved including the Conservative and Unionist Women's Franchise Association, the Women's Liberal Association, the Men's League for Women's Suffrage, the Liverpool University Women's Suffrage Society, the Birkenhead and Wirral Suffrage Societies, the Liverpool Women's Suffrage Society, the Women's Temperance Association and the Independent Labour Party. It is interesting to note that the WSPU seems not to have been part of the event, at least according to the newspaper.

Among the speakers on the platforms were Miss Rathbone, Mrs. Allan Bright, Mrs. Stewart Brown, Mr. John Edwards and sympathetic local M.P.s. At the end of the afternoon the usual resolution in favour of voting rights for women was moved by Mrs. Selina Cooper and carried by an overwhelming majority 'only three or four hands in all were held up against it'. For the afternoon a 'motor-procession' had been organised for which motors had been lent, 'by Conservatives, Liberals, ILP and suffragists and which had been decorated in their respective colours'.[9] It would be interesting to know who in the ILP was in possession of a motor-car in those days!

The Liverpool Women's Social and Political Union

On the basis of information gathered from *Votes for Women* as well as the local newspapers the WSPU membership in

9 *LC,* 20.6.1910, p.7.
10 P.J. Waller, *Democracy and Sectarianism. A political and social history of Liverpool 1868 - 1939.* Liverpool, 1981, p.503.
11 *Votes for Women (VFW),* June, 1909.

Selina Cooper addressing the crowd on St George's Plateau. Note the Liverpool banner behind her.

Patricia Woodlock

Liverpool seems to have been quite diverse. In trying to assess it one should remember that only the names of the activists have survived in records, which tells us little about the women, especially working class women, who sympathised with the movement but could not afford to become actively involved. Nevertheless it seems that in Liverpool, where most upper class women concerned with women's suffrage were tied up with the LWSS, the WSPU was able to attract the active support of women with trade union connections and white collar workers. In addition there was a mixture of students, artists and women who moved in the more Bohemian circles of Liverpool.

Alice Morrisey, wife of the Labour councillor John W.T. Morrissey has already been mentioned. She was involved with the ILP and the Co-operative Movement in Liverpool and perhaps co-founder of the LWSPU.[10] Mrs. Myer was a regular speaker at open air meetings and was arrested as a member of the deputation to Prime Minister Asquith in June 1909. On that occasion *Votes for Women* wrote that she was '...sacrificing the companionship of a devoted husband and three children in order to do her part'.[11] Her husband was an electrical engineer, and one can speculate whether it is through him that the LWSPU in its early days was able to meet in the building of the Engineers Union on Mount Pleasant. Another activist was Mrs. Bessie Morris who for a while wrote the local news from Liverpool for *Votes For Women*. She was arrested during the same delegation to Asquith as Mrs. Myer, she too spoke at numerous open air meetings. Georgina Healiss was one of five daughters of a local shoe and boot maker. She was arrested whilst causing a disturbance during the visit of a cabinet minister to Liverpool in 1909 and *Votes for Women* wrote that she '...has been for three years in the movement and has a mother equally enthusiastic, who does her part by looking after the child of one of those who took part in the deputation. She is looking forward to a *glorious victory*'.[12] There is evidence that in 1912 old Mrs. Healiss was arrested on the same window smashing raid as Dr. Alice Ker.

Of a different background was Liverpool's best known activist at the time, **Patricia Woodlock**. Her father, David Woodlock, was a successful, self-taught artist of whom the Walker Art Gallery in Liverpool has works in its collection. Patricia became involved with women's suffrage first in Manchester and later in Liverpool. She was an untiring and audacious campaigner who spoke at numerous occasions up and down the country. In 1909 she was imprisoned for the fourth time for taking part in militant action and given three months in Holloway Prison. On her release a journalist of the *Liverpool Courier* wrote: 'She is a Liverpool girl, refined, tender-hearted, heroic'. To subject her to solitary confinement for seventy-seven days was 'like taking a bludgeon to break a butterfly'. The National WSPU issued a postcard with Patricia's portrait in recognition of her contribution to the movement. Examining the sources one could come to think that the WSPU generated more activity than the NUWSS. This impression is not accurate. Although the NUWSS did not particularly shun publicity, it did not see it as a major weapon in the struggle. The WSPU on the contrary left no opportunity unused to make headlines. In actual fact what appears a different *amount* of activity is more a different *kind* of activity. This was particularly so in Liverpool. Here the WSPU started off as an organisation which received its instructions from outside the city. It had to work very hard to build up a profile and did so by taking to the streets and going for the more spectacular events which would draw the attention of the public at large. Since the Liverpool WSPU membership, with a few exceptions, did not have contacts in high places, lobbying of important people or petitioning was not seen as a priority.

Education
Like the LWSS, the WSPU saw educating people about the issue of women's suffrage as important but had a somewhat different approach.

12 *VFW*, June 1909, p.877.
13 *LDP&M*, 22.12.1908, p.9.
14 *LC*, 22.12.1908, p.7.
15 *LC*, 13.2.1909, p.8.

During spring and summer open air meetings would be held. On weekdays speakers would go to factory gates to address the workers during their dinner hour. On Saturdays and Sundays they could be found where people went for their recreation: in the public parks or on the sands of Southport and New Brighton. Then there were the regular 'At Homes' already mentioned, at first in the building of the Engineers Association at 48, Mount Pleasant, later on in the WSPU's own premises. These meetings were both for non-members who wanted to find out more about women's suffrage as well as for regular members to discuss the campaign's progress. There would always be a speaker, often from outside, followed by debate.

Mass meetings and demonstrations

The WSPU was extremely skilled in organising events which would attract a mass audience. A much favoured spot for open air meetings was St. George's Plateau, which was in the centre of the city and could accommodate large crowds. For indoor meetings the Sun Hall in Kensington became the WSPU's favourite meeting place.

Ada Flatman, the first paid organiser for the WSPU in Liverpool. She is wearing her prison brooch.

In December 1908 the Chancellor Lloyd George was to speak at a Liberal Rally in Liverpool. Preparations for a 'warm welcome' were master-minded by the WSPU with the assistance of two members from outside who would soon be spending more time in the city; Mary Phillips from Scotland and Ada Flatman from London.

The Chancellor, who had suffered his share of disruption by suffragettes at meetings elsewhere, had made it clear before his arrival in Liverpool that he would no longer address audiences at which ladies were present. The Liberal Party in Liverpool had to choose between him and the women. He got his way, and the *Daily Post* which claimed that between five and six thousand Liverpool men had packed the Sun Hall wrote: 'Many loyal Liberal women were deprived of the privilege of listening to the Chancellor of the Exchequer's speech because prudence dictated the necessity of keeping from the hall the suffragette black sheep'.[13] But Lloyd George's decision was accepted by the Liberal women in Liverpool as shown in an open letter to him published by the *Liverpool Courier*. In this letter the Women's Liberal Association rejected the tactics of the militant suffragettes and accepted the need for the exclusion of all women from the rally. Confidence in Lloyd George as the 'trusted champion' of women's equality was restated and the letter signed by all the secretaries of the Women's Liberal Association, several of whom were also leaders of the LWSS.[14]

A WSPU rally opposite the Empire Theatre. Patricia Woodlock is speaking with the Liscard banner just visible behind her.

If there were no suffragettes inside the hall during the rally, they were unmistakenly present outside. Four women wearing sashes of the WSPU drove in an open carriage to and fro in front of the hall, delivering short speeches by megaphone to the ever growing, cheering crowd. When the carriage was prevented from approaching the hall again, the women stepped off and two of them, the local Patricia Woodlock and Helen Tolson from Manchester were promptly arrested and taken to Prescot Street Police Station. They were released on

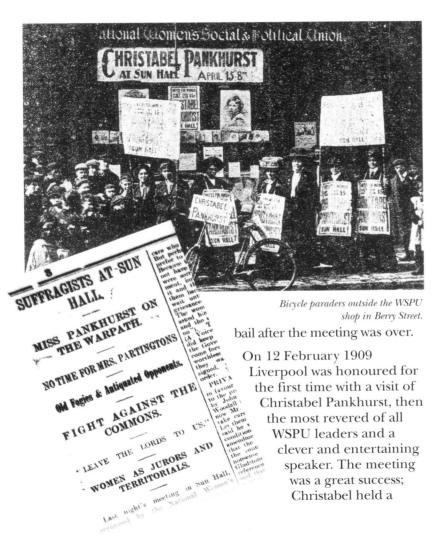

Bicycle paraders outside the WSPU shop in Berry Street.

bail after the meeting was over.

On 12 February 1909 Liverpool was honoured for the first time with a visit of Christabel Pankhurst, then the most revered of all WSPU leaders and a clever and entertaining speaker. The meeting was a great success; Christabel held a

rousing speech which was reported at length by the local newspapers and the event resulted in a 'phenomenal demand for membership cards'.[15] A piquant detail of this visit is that Christabel was the guest of Mrs. Allan Bright, still a leading lady in the LWSS. Mrs. Bright's husband, in his role of secretary of the Liverpool Liberal Party, had chaired rallies and meetings which had been severely disrupted by members of the LWSPU and one wonders how he felt about having the fierce young leader of the enemy organisation under his roof ! In April 1910, she visited Liverpool again and this time the event was advertised in the striking manner characteristic of the WSPU by means of a bicycle parade and a living letter-parade, whereby WSPU members walked the street each carrying a placard with on letter of their heroine's name.

Militancy

In London Mrs. Pankhurst had developed a type of meeting which attracted large numbers of women and which became an effective recruiting ground for new activists. Since women could not vote and thus had no voice in the Parliament of the land, the WSPU in London organised mass meetings of women to discuss matters of importance called 'Women's Parliaments'. The standard format for such meetings was to have one or more star speakers including one of the Pankhursts, and then to discuss and pass a resolution to the Government. Women in the audience would be invited to form a delegation to the Prime Minister to present the resolution. Since the Prime Minister was refusing to see any suffragettes, those who volunteered knew they would have to fight for access and run the risk of being arrested in the process.

In March 1909 Liverpool held its own Women's Parliament in the Sun Hall, with Mrs. Pankhurst as main speaker. At this meeting several Liverpool women volunteered for the deputation to Prime Minister Asquith, planned for the 30th March. They were Mrs. Hilton, Miss Broughton, Patricia Woodlock, Mrs. Bessie Morris and Alice Burton. In the event all five were arrested during the skirmishes which followed when they were refused entry to see the Prime Minister. They declined to pay a fine and were given one month's imprisonment in Holloway.

16 *VFW*, June 1909, front page.

Released prisoners touring the streets of Liverpool.

VICTORY

LANCASHIRE

DREADNOUGHT W.S.P.U

WELCOME.

HOLLOWAY

JAIL.

Taken into Dock, March 31st 1909.
Ready for Active Service, June 16th 190:

A PATRIOT.

*How 'Votes For Women' portrayed Patricia Woodlock's
imprisonment in Holloway.*

Patricia Woodlock, because of her previous convictions, was given three months.

As had become tradition with the WSPU the prisoners were given a grand reception when they returned to Liverpool after their release. There was a tour in an open landau through the centre of town complete with colour bearer (Georgina Healiss), drum band and a contingent of local WSPU members dressed in white, green and purple.

Patricia Woodlock, after her three months spell in Holloway, received special honours. The front page of *Votes for Women* carried a cartoon illustrating Patricia's release from Holloway.[16]

In August 1909 one of the Liberal Cabinet Ministers, Haldane, came to Liverpool to speak about the Budget in the Sun Hall. Interruption of Liberal meetings by WSPU-activists had become a pattern and in anticipation the *Liverpool Courier* had sent its reporter to the Sun Hall. He described how, although no suffragettes had been allowed into the meeting, Haldane's speech was interrupted rather noisily by the breaking of the hall's window panes. When the police went outside to inspect the building they didn't see any thing until '... suddenly the frail figure of a little woman peered out from behind a chimney stack at the back on a Kensington street building, an arm was raised and fell, and crash went another window'. It turned out that the suffragettes, knowing that they would be thrown out of the hall as soon as they raised their voices, had decided to attack from the outside. They had hired an empty house opposite and from its roof attacked the windows of the hall. When they knew the police had spotted them they decided to make the best use of the time left before they were arrested and '... slates began to fall from the roof into the entry below, where the police were gathering and while the progress of officers was in this way hampered, good use was being made of megaphones. The familiar cry rang out *Votes for Women...*'. The reporter described how the woman handled her unusual ammunition 'with a dexterity which was nothing short of marvellous' and how she and her comrades were eventually brought down from the roof by the police, an exercise watched by the crowd down below with a great deal of amusement.[17] Seven women were arrested and taken to the local police station.

When they refused to be bound over they were put in Walton Prison pending a further hearing in the Police Court. Once 'inside' they proceeded to break the windows of their cells with their boots, to sing suffragette songs and '...generally behave in what is described as a mutinous manner'.[18] In Court the next day they were charged with wilful damage and assault of the police. After the hearing, during which the women conducted their own defence, the Magistrate sentenced them to one or two months imprisonment in the second division, i.e. the division used for ordinary criminals. Georgina Healiss's arguments that they should be dealt with as political prisoners and be put in the first division were not accepted. The women were then conducted into a Black Maria parked in the police yard at Hatton Garden and driven off to Walton Prison. Before the van had left the yard one of them managed to smash the narrow glass panel in its door, much to the delight of the crowd of sympathisers who had gathered for the hearing. In the afternoon an ad hoc protest meeting was organised at Wellington Column, presided over by Jessica Walker, a Liverpool artist and supporter

17 *LC*,21.8.1909.
18 *LC*,24.8.1909.
19 *VFW*, 27.8.1909,
p.111.
20 *LC*, 18.7.1910, p.5

of the WSPU. She told the crowd that she herself was on remand having been arrested during a deputation to the House of Commons. That same night some 200 to 300 people were addressed by Miss Broughton, Mrs. Myer and Mrs. Morris, outside Walton Gaol. Later on it transpired that the prisoners had gone on hunger strike prior to their court appearance and had continued with this action for five days until the authorities, worried about the state of their health, released them before they had completed their sentence. The *Liverpool Courier* reported the whole affair extensively and mentioned that Mrs. Jennie Baines, a seasoned suffragette from Manchester, had taken charge of the prisoners after their release and that a doctor, Mary Davies, had been engaged to monitor their progress.

On the whole, the *Liverpool Courier* reported with good humour and sympathy, unlike the *Liverpool Daily Post* which took a very unsympathetic stance: 'Seven viragos have given a lesson to the country which it will not be slow to

profit by, and we trust that the arm of the outraged justice will administer to them a lesson which they will not soon forget. A body which, to gratify the morbid vanity of its members, will seriously endanger the lives of hundreds of their fellow creatures, is a nuisance and a danger which must be dealt with firmly and promptly'.[19]

A month after the other women's suffrage organisations in Liverpool had held their mass demonstration on St. George's Plateau in June 1910, the WSPU held its own in the same place. This time there were four lorries serving as platforms for the speakers. The meeting was opened by Mrs. Avery, 'a well known resident from Huyton' and active member of the WSPU, followed by Mrs. Mahood from the Wallasey Branch. The Socialist John Edwards, a member of Liverpool ILP, also spoke and gave a very competent outline of women's inequality in Britain. He expressed the hope that the audience would show 'that Liverpool, at least, was in favour of the franchise for women'.[20]

4

WITH IMAGINATION!

As elsewhere in the country the campaign for the vote in Liverpool was characterised by its liveliness, spiritedness and imaginative ideas which encouraged the involvement of large numbers of women, on different levels.

The Shopfront

Soon after the national WSPU had sent Ada Flatman to Liverpool as paid organiser she proposed the opening of a shop as a base for the organisation. This was not a novel idea as the WSPU already had shops elsewhere, in London and Oldham for example. A shop functioned as the organisation's meeting room, drop-in centre for casual callers, distribution place for publicity and as a centre for fundraising activities.[1] The WSPU's first shop in Liverpool was at 28 Berry Street. Its official opening had to be postponed because the decorating undertaken by the members themselves had not been finished in time. It finally took place at the end of September 1909 and a local woman, Mrs. Doris (or Dorice) Callender, became the first shopworker. It quickly became the centre of activity for the Liverpool WSPU. According to her diary Dr. Ker visited it for the first time on the 13th of October, a mere fortnight after the opening and subsequently went there at least once, sometimes twice a week, to meet the organiser or to collect her quota of 'Votes for Women' to sell. She also occasionally minded the shop to give the regular worker a break.

In April 1910 Mrs. Pethick Lawrence, the National Treasurer of the WSPU wrote a letter to Ada who apparently had asked approval for moving the shop from Berry Street to Renshaw Street. Why she proposed this is not clear but Mrs. Pethick Lawrence did not object although she warned Ada against incurring unnecessary expenditure. (The letter is all the more interesting as it makes reference to the money raised by the WSPU in Liverpool for the campaign and the cost of running it).[2] The move took place and in March 1911 the WSPU was installed at 11 Renshaw Street. The rooms had been made to look cosy with furniture, furnishings and watercolours donated by members.

When eventually Helen Jollie was appointed as the WSPU's third organiser the WSPU moved again. From January 1913 its offices, now no longer

Notes
1 A letter from Mrs Pethick Lawrence to Ada Flatman concerning the opening of a shop in Liverpool is transcribed in Appendix 1.
2 This letter is transcribed in Appendix 1.
3 VFW, 31.3.1911.

with a shopfront, could be found in Canning Chambers, 2 South John Street where they remained until the organisation disappeared in 1914.

The 1911 Census

A good opportunity for the WSPU's ingenuity in the search for new weapons was offered by the census scheduled for March 1911. In Liverpool Ada Flatman had resigned as paid organiser and had been replaced by Alice Davies. It fell to her to co-ordinate in Liverpool the nationwide 'census evasion' master-minded by the WSPU. The simple idea underlying the action was that of citizenship. If the purpose of the census was to gather useful information about all British citizens then women need not co-operate with the exercise as they were not considered to be citizens, i.e. people worthy of the right to vote. Clearly this refusal to co-operate was intended as a publicity stunt, a piece of action in which many women could take part as it did not involve any physical violence. All that participants were asked to do was to spoil their census paper or to be away from home on the day the census enumerator was to visit

to take details. Thus they would not figure in the census results and, if the action was widespread enough this would seriously invalidate the whole exercise. The actual forms of the 1911 census are still subject to the 100 years disclosure rule, which means that not until the year 2011 will we be able to establish how many and which women took part in the action. From the pages of *Votes for Women* in March 1911 we get glimpses of activity on Merseyside: 'Liverpool plans are not made public. Members should apply to Miss Davies' and 'A large number of names are coming in for the Census Protest. On Thursday, April 6, members will meet in their new office, 11 Renshaw Street, to take tea and talk over their experiences on April 2.'[3]

Most of the organisation of the protest centred on helping women to be 'absent from home' on the evening of the enumerator's visit, as for many this was not as simple as it may be today. Women activists who lived in larger houses were asked to make these available for so called 'census-parties', i.e. to offer a safe place for 'resisters' to come and spend the night.

The *Liverpool Echo* in its article on the result of the census mentions the 'Suffragette Boycott' and talks about the 'All Night Social', 'Boisterous Scenes' and 'Sleeping out in Private Houses' in London and Edinburgh. With regards to Liverpool the paper notes: 'The suffragettes of Liverpool and district had on the occasion of the census a "field night", the object in view being to defeat the census as an act of retaliation upon the Government because of their attitude towards women's suffrage. The campaign for midnight Sunday-Monday, April 2-3 - be it chronologically set out - was well managed, under the skilful

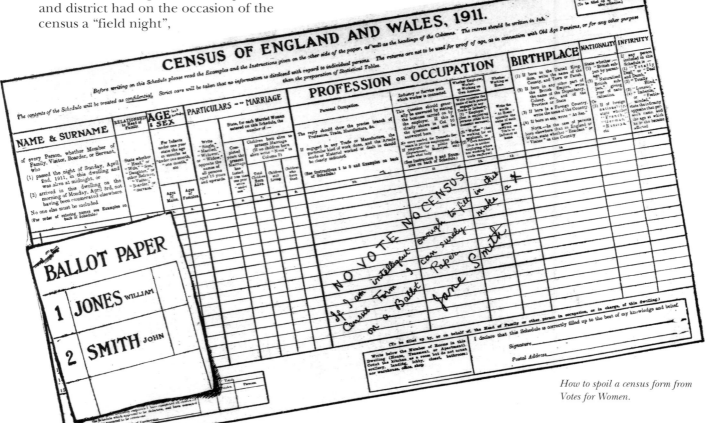

How to spoil a census form from Votes for Women.

4 Liverpool Echo, 3.4.1911, p.5.

tactician, Miss Davies, who has taken over the control of the local work of the WSPU since the departure of the rosy and resonant Miss Flaxman (*sic*) for Cheltenham. Three great rendezvous were selected for the occasion of these secret lady moonlighters in which the elite of the suffragette stalwarts of Liverpool and district gathered at the dead of night. Many came from a distance, some from Ireland and some from Scotland (in Liverpool for a double event), but most of them were dwellers on the Mersey banks - both sides.'[4]

After the event the *Birkenhead News* wrote on 5 April under the headline 'Lady Dodgers: A large furnished house in James Street, Birkenhead was engaged for a week, and thither on Sunday night there resorted a large number of ladies, including many from Liverpool, determined to add their voice to the protest from all over the country, until the house was packed with evaders. During their stay they had three hearty meals, and the time was passed in friendly chat and sleep. Those for whom there was no rest on beds, sofas or chairs, sleeping in true Bohemian fashion on the floor. Across the census form for the house it was written that there were no 'persons' in the house, only 'a few women' for the reason for this census protest is that women are not 'persons' in the eyes of the law. The other 'official' houses where evaders gathered were at Liscard and Waterloo, at the residences of Miss Hoy and Miss Hall respectively. Miss Davies says that although the resisters were very tired when the night was over, they had a good time.' This information from the *Birkenhead News*, although it captures the spirit of the events, is not quite correct. The house in James Street was No. 6 and the private home of Dr. Ker, who made the following notes in her diary: Tuesday, 28 March. 'In the evening Margaret and I went to lecture by Joseph Clayton on Census resistance at Hardman Hall. Not home till after 11.' Sunday, 2 April. 'Census evaders here all night, 57 of them. Tea soon after midnight.' Monday, 3 April. 'Lay on floor of Mary's room for abt. an hour till 2.30, all other rooms and floors being occupied. A meal abt. 3.30, Miss Ross and Miss Abraham left at 5.30, others later on. Miss Davies, Mrs. Wallace and Mrs. Gray at bkft.' It is not difficult to picture the situation!

Margaret Ker

The Pageant

The WSPU's ability to develop ever new ways of drawing people's attention to the campaign and of getting more women to take an active part in it is well illustrated by the event staged in February 1912. The writer and actress Cicily Hamilton, member of the Actresses' Franchise League, had written a theatrical spectacle called 'Pageant of Great Women'. This production was woven round women whose names were known to history - from Sappho to Jane Austen and from Bodicea to Grace Darling. It was simple in structure and had a large number of parts. It was staged by women's suffrage branches up and down the country both to entertain and educate local people. In February 1912 it was staged in Liverpool in the Philharmonic Hall on the occasion of yet another visit by Mrs. Pankhurst. The producer was Edith Craig, daughter of the famous actress Ellen Terry and many Liverpool women took part in it, splendidly dressed up in appropriate costume. The event was a great success and the play was also staged in Birkenhead where Dr. Alice Ker played the part of Saint Theresa and her daughter Margaret that of Flora McDonald.

Under the Organ

Some members of the WSPU went to great length to bring the women's demand to the attention of the Government.

Mary Phillips, the Scottish suffragette who spent some time in Liverpool as temporary paid organiser, made the local headlines in April 1909. On Saturday 10th, the M.P. and Chief Secretary of Ireland, Mr. Birtell, was to receive an honorary degree during a ceremony in St. George's Hall. On Friday evening, passing by the Hall and noticing one of the doors open, Mary Phillips slipped inside, and while somebody was playing the organ, hid herself

5 L.D.P. & M.
12.4.1909.
6 Common Cause, Vol.
1, December 1909.

under the judge's desk in the assize court. Here she stayed until the Hall was closed later on in the evening. There she spent the night, somewhat hungry but not uncomfortable. When the morning came, before the custodians arrived to open up, she hid herself underneath the platform on which the degree ceremony was to take place. As she told a reporter of the *Liverpool Daily Post* later on, she was so far stuck down 'that when Mr. Birtell was receiving his doctorate and when I began to scream in favour of the vote for women, the police had jolly hard work to find me. They groped about and shouted, struck matches and drew batons to protect their heads against striking stanchions or props, and at last they found me'. And she continued 'I could not help laughing at all the fuss. Fancy a woman creating all this stir and giving such trouble. But you know, (...) that is what we mean to do until our victory is secure.'[5] Imagine this bizarre incident in the solemn, awe-inspiring surroundings of St. George's Hall!

Election Tactics

In 1910 several elections took place in Liverpool in which both suffragettes and suffragists were heavily involved. It is worthwhile to look briefly at these events as they give a good illustration of how the issues were tackled at local level.

As a lead up to the General Election in January, Merseyside began to receive visits from leading Liberal politicians including Winston Churchill and the Prime Minister, Asquith, all during December 1909. The Labour Party also took part in the elections, with Alexander Cameron, an active supporter of women's suffrage, as Labour candidate for the Kirkdale constituency.

The LWSS became very active under the leadership of Eleanor Rathbone, who was thoroughly familiar with traditional political campaigning. She established a campaigning committee in each electoral division to organise meetings and petitions. For example, on 17 December a 'small but enthusiastic meeting' was held in the Everton Division and on the 21st of that month the last of a series of preparatory meetings was held at the Mill Street Mission Hall (West Toxteth) where, 'in spite of atrocious weather, quite a good audience turned up to hear Mrs. Allan Bright, Cllr. E. Rathbone, Mr. Hugh Rathbone and Mr. Darbyshire.'[6]

The line the LWSS took in this election campaign was to inform the (male) voters of the position of candidates on women's suffrage and to advise them to vote for those who were in favour, regardless of their party-political allegiance. On the 2nd January the *Liverpool Courier* published a letter signed by Mrs. Fawcett, the President of the National Union, which summed up the position of the Liverpool candidates. In a letter to the *Courier* on the 7th January, Eleanor Rathbone asked for helpers to collect signatures for a voters' petition in favour of women's enfranchisement. Anyone interested was invited to become involved and on polling day to turn up at one of the committee rooms at 36 Lord Street, 94 Smithdown Road or 247 Stanley Road.

This solid but traditional way of electioneering was in total contrast to the action of the WSPU branches on Merseyside. It was by now national policy of the WSPU to oppose *all* Liberal candidates, regardless of their own individual position on women's suffrage, in a bid to force the Liberal Government to change its position. There was the usual round of open air meetings, many at factory gates, which attracted large crowds. There was a stream of propaganda including a poster campaign issued from the vantage point of the shop in 28 Berry Street and events such as the driving of a decorated motor car through town, 'with the large Double-Face Asquith on the back'.[7] Much more spectacular, however, were the interruptions of the visits of the Liberal leaders to Merseyside during election time. In Southport the local WSPU had prepared for Winston Churchill's speaking engagement on 6th December 1909 at the Empire Hall. Despite extensive police precautions Churchill's speech was interrupted by voices from the outside. It appeared that three women had clambered onto the roof of the hall the night before and had spent the entire night up there (in December!) in order to be able to disrupt the meeting. Dora Marsden, secretary of Southport WSPU, Helen Tolson from Manchester and a Miss Winson Etherley were brought down from the roof and taken to the police station. It is not clear from the local newspaper whether they were charged or not.[8]

7 VFW, December 1909, p.219.
8 Southport Visiter, 16.12.1909.
9 C. Lytton, Prisons and Prisoners. Some personal experiences, London, 1914, p.235-295. See also the C. Lytton Papers in the Liverpool Central Library Records Office.

At the same time the Prime Minister visited Liverpool to deliver an important speech at the Reform Club, the local Liberal Party Club. As a precaution the police had taken possession of all the offices in the neighbourhood and detectives had been placed on the rooftops of adjoining buildings. According to the *Daily Post* the police were especially on the look out for suffragettes, 'close upon a dozen of them were in the vicinity, but the police kept them under close observation, and as they walked up and down in couples in front of the club, each couple was followed at close range by two detective officers'. Despite this vigilance some of the women managed to break through the cordon on the Prime Minister's arrival and shout slogans. Then a woman, dressed as an orange-seller, threw something into the Prime Minister's motor car. It turned out to be no more than an empty ginger beer bottle which landed on the front seat without doing any damage. The woman was arrested together with her companion and taken to the main Bridewell where they were 'booked in' as Leslie Hall and Selina Martin, both from London. They were remanded for seven days for inquiries and although this meant that they would be in gaol over Christmas, an application for bail was refused. A week later they were sentenced to one month's imprisonment in Walton Gaol. During that period several demonstrations and meetings organised by Ada Flatman and others outside the prison attracted considerable crowds. The WSPU used this imprisonment as a focal point for anti-Liberal Government activity and Lady Constance Lytton's arrest and subsequent hunger strike during the same period made much bigger headlines than all the campaigning of the LWSS put together. This incident has been extensively documented in the suffrage literature and by Constance Lytton herself.[9] A member of a leading aristocratic family, Constance had become involved with the WSPU through Christabel Pankhurst. In October 1909 she had been arrested in Newcastle for throwing a stone at a minister's car and sent to prison there. She went on hunger strike and after medical examination the prison doctors advised that Constance's heart was too weak for her to stand forced feeding. Two days later she was released but she was convinced that her aristocratic background had been as much a consideration for this early release as her heart condition. In January 1910 disguised as a seamstress, she took part in the demonstration outside Liverpool's Walton Gaol, and when she was arrested gave her name as 'Jane Warton'. Again she went on hunger strike but the doctors declared her fit enough to be force fed without bothering to examine her. When a few days later the Prison Governor did find out about her real identity she was released 'for health reasons'. For Constance and for the WSPU these events provided proof that the government had two types of treatment for prisoners; one for the rich and one for the poor. This of course was strenuously denied by the Government.

The death of a local Conservative M.P. for Kirkdale caused a by-election in July 1910. The candidate for the Conservative Party, Colonel Kyffin-Taylor, stood 'For God, for King and for Liberty'. Alexander Cameron, who stood as candidate for the Labour Party as he had done in January, promoted social reform. The by-election coincided with the passing of another Women's Suffrage Bill in Parliament and there

was much agitation by the Liverpool women's suffrage organisations in support of this Bill. However, both the LWSS and LWSPU plunged into local election activities. It is not clear which line WSPU speakers took this time when addressing local voters, but the LWSS had certainly done its homework. In a letter to the editor of the *Daily Post and Mercury* Eleanor Rathbone asked for support for Mr. Cameron 'who declared himself in unequivocal terms in favour of women's suffrage in his election address and has pledged himself to support the bill for the enfranchisement of women occupants'.[10] She admitted that Colonel Kyffin-Taylor had stated to be in favour of a limited parliamentary vote for women but: 'As, however, he refused to

Constance Lytton disguised as Jane Warton

10 L.D.P. & M.,
14.7.1910.

repeat this statement in his election address, or to pledge himself to vote for the bill, we are obliged, by the rules of the National Union, to support the candidate who has done both these things'. She invited all Liberal women to come to the committee room the LWSS had opened up in 19 Kirkdale Road and to work for the Labour candidate.

Despite this support the Conservative candidate won with a modest majority.

In front of the LWSS election office at 19, Kirkdale Road

5

FROM SUFFRAGIST TO MILITANT SUFFRAGETTE DR. ALICE KER

Alice Ker (seated on the left) and friends about 1875

Although this booklet's main aim is to celebrate all women who made a contribution to the campaign on Merseyside, there are several reasons to single out Dr. Alice Ker.

The most obvious one is the existence of material (although unpublished) which contains what appears to be the only known first hand account of aspects of the campaign on Merseyside. The second reason is that she started off as a suffragist, a member of the Birkenhead branch of the NWSS, but after some twelve years 'crossed the floor' and joined the WSPU, which she supported until the vote was won. The third reason is that although Dr. Ker in terms of background, education and social status was representative of one class of women who worked for 'The Cause', she was at the same time an unusual individual whose life deserves to be recorded in more detail.

Background

Alice Jane Shannon Ker was born in 1853, the eldest of nine children of Edward Stewart Ker, Free Church Minister in Deskford, a tiny parish in

Notes

1 Stevenson, L., *Recollection of the Public Works and Home Life of Louisa and Flora Stevenson.* Ediburgh 1914.

2 A.J.S.Ker, The beginnings of a memoir (1853 - 1880). Typescript in private collection.

Banffshire, Scotland. By the time she emerged as a member of the Birkenhead Women's Suffrage Society (BWSS) she was a practising G.P., the thirteenth woman to have had her name placed on the British Medical Register. In the first instance it seems difficult to understand how a minister's daughter from a remote Scottish village was able to gain access to a profession so determined to keep women out, but a closer look at her background provides some answers. Alice Ker's maternal grandfather, James Stevenson, was a successful Glasgow business man, who became the founder of Jarrow Chemical Works at South Shields. He had eleven children, Alice's mother being the eldest of six girls. Four of them remained unmarried and lived together in Edinburgh, where their home became a centre for intellectual and social life. Louise and Flora Stevenson, especially, were engaged in public work of the most varied nature. The latter was also a member of the Society for Women's Suffrage and Vice-President of the Women's Liberal Unionist Association in Edinburgh.[1] Of her own mother Dr. Ker wrote '... my Mother must have been a born feminist, for even as long ago as that she always said that her boys should not have more chances than her girls, who should be brought up to earn their living like the boys.'[2] Although Alice's early formal education was rather patchy, she received ample education through her contact with the progressive and prosperous homes of numerous aunts and uncles scattered over Scotland and the north of England. She often stayed with the Edinburgh aunts and must have absorbed many progressive ideas of the day almost automatically. In 1872 she started to attend University Classes for Ladies in literature and physiology and met the women students who, led by Sophia Jex-Blake, were trying to secure medical training in Edinburgh and decided that she too wanted to become a doctor. In her autobiographical notes she wrote: 'This was partly hereditary, for my Mother always said that if she had been a boy she would have been a surgeon in the Navy'.[2] She faced all the obstacles in the way of women who wanted to qualify as doctors: even though they might have successfully studied all necessary subjects on an extramural basis, Edinburgh University was unwilling to award them degrees. However, when the Irish colleges opened their examinations to women in 1879 she obtained the Licentiate of the King's and Queen's College of Physicians, Ireland. During the decade that followed she built up her experience - she shared a practice with Sophia Jex-Blake in Edinburgh for a year, spent a year in Switzerland studying at Berne University (paid for by Aunt Louisa), worked as a House-Surgeon in the Children's Hospital in Birmingham, ran a practice in Leeds and in 1887 returned to Edinburgh to set up an independent practice.

In 1888 she married her cousin, Edward Ker, a shipping merchant in Liverpool and settled with him in Birkenhead. Although Alice never became to Birkenhead society what the Stevenson aunts were to Edinburgh, she developed a wide range of social contacts and joined a number of public organisations. She was helped in this by being a woman doctor and was soon consulted by several leading ladies on Merseyside. She became a Honorary Medical Officer to the Wirral Hospital for Sick Children, and to the

MOTHERHOOD:

A

BOOK FOR EVERY WOMAN.

BY

DR. ALICE KER

(MRS. STEWART KER),

OF BIRKENHEAD,

AUTHOR OF "LECTURES TO WOMEN,"

Hon. Medical Officer to the Wirral Hospital for Sick Children, and to the Birkenhead Lying-In Hospital.

JOHN HEYWOOD,
DEANSGATE AND RIDGEFIELD, MANCHESTER;
1, PATERNOSTER BUILDINGS,
LONDON.

Birkenhead Lying-In Hospital. Alice kept a fairly accurate record of her social engagements, the more splendid of which included receptions at the Town Hall and garden parties given by families such as the Brocklebanks and Bibbys.

Soon she widened her range of 'good works'. In 1898 she lectured to 'ladies' attending courses run by the Manchester School of Domestic Economy. It was on request of these students that in 1891 she published a book called *Motherhood: A Book For Every Woman*, in which she dealt with female adolescence, marriage, pregnancy and childcare in a manner considerably more open, forthright and progressive than similar texts of the period. She became involved with the Temperance movement and the Society for the Prevention of Cruelty to Animals and from time to time attended meetings of the Peace Society.

Suffragist

Although Alice was familiar with the suffrage scene in Edinburgh, she was relatively slow to catch up with the movement in Birkenhead. Her first ref-erence to it is in March 1891, when she wrote in her diary: 'Wrote Suffrage letter to Daily Post in morning'. Whatever the letter was about, it wasn't published by the paper. In 1894 she became friendly with Miss Jeannie Willmer and Miss Dismore and together they began to expand local suffrage activity along NUWSS lines. During 1895 there was a series of Women's Suffrage meetings, mainly in the homes of the Misses Mellor or Dalby and in November they held a very successful public meeting. Despite the loss of her first child and the birth of two girls, Margaret Louise and Mary Dunlop, Alice kept in touch and attended all important events. In 1897, for example, she was at a Public Meeting in Southport Town Hall where she could renew her acquaintance with the guest speaker, Isabella Ford, whom she knew from the time she practised in Leeds. The Birkenhead Society's activities seemed to decrease during the years 1900 - 1904, which corresponds with a lull in activity of the NUWSS nationally, but Alice made new contacts through the movement nevertheless. Thus Mrs. Carmichael Stopes (Mary Stopes) of Family Planning fame, was the guest speaker at the Annual meeting of the BWSS in 1903 and when a year later she returned to speak in Hoylake, she stayed at Dr. Ker's. The two women kept in touch and in later years Dr. Ker would visit Mrs. Stopes when in London.

Judging by the notes in her diary, by 1908 things began to change for Alice. In May 1907 her husband had died unexpectedly. She had shared a lot of activities with him - sport, socializing, travel - and his death must have left her with a gap to fill. It may also have left her freer to make the kind of contacts she was really interested in. In addition to existing activities Alice visited the Clarion Club in Liverpool attending lectures by George Bernard Shaw or Russell Smart - the latter spoke on 'A Man's Thoughts on Women'! She met Mrs. Jeannie Mole from Bebington, the Fabian activist and untiring promotor of trade unions for women and became quite friendly with her. She was not present at the first public meeting of Christabel Pankhurst in Liverpool in 1909 but in February of that year she noted that the Temperance Society had a suffrage meeting and that Patricia Woodlock, 'from Liverpool', was the speaker. In May she went to a meeting

with Mrs. Forbes Robertson, national WSPU speaker, and must have made personal contact as the latter's private address is down in Alice's diary for that year. So is that of Mary Gawthorpe, the powerful regional organiser for the WSPU from Manchester. On 8 June Alice and her friend Miss Wyse, secretary of the BWSS, went to an 'At Home' of the WSPU where Mary Gawthorpe and Miss Flatman unfolded plans for a festive reception for Patricia Woodlock, about to be released after a three months spell in prison. A few days later Alice visited friends where she met Mrs. Cobden Sanderson, member of the WSPU's national leadership, as well as Mr. Lyon Blease, Liverpool University lecturer and member of the Men's League for Women's Suffrage.[3] These contacts must have had an impact on Alice as on 21 June she noted: 'Did up all neces-

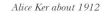

Alice Ker about 1912

3 W. Lyon Blease, *Against Prejudice.* 1910.
4 This fact is not mentioned in Constance Lytton's *Prisons and Prisoners* although she mentions contacting Dr.Ker when she was released from Walton Gaol.

sary work in morning, and in afternoon Margaret and I went over to Liverpool to meet Miss Patricia Woodlock. Margaret helped to draw her carriage and I to carry the banner. Speaking from a lorry in front of St. George's Hall.' And the next day: 'Margaret and I went to Miss Woodlock's reception at the Yamen Cafe'. Late of getting home'. In the course of a year Alice and her daughter Margaret, now seventeen, had changed from suffragists into suffragettes.

Suffragette
This change had been gradual because Alice's close friends did not follow her into the WSPU. For a little while she maintained two circles of friends, with rather opposing views on strategies for the campaign. For example, she had Miss Wyse, Miss Mary Gawthorpe and Mrs. Forbes Robertson for a late dinner the day after several Liverpool and Southport suffragettes had been arrested for window smashing in London. The relative merits of lawful and militant struggle must have been hotly discussed, even if in a ladylike fashion. A week later Alice gave an open air speech at a public meeting on St.

George's Plateau for the Men's League which supported both suffragists and suffragettes but by October 1909 her contact with the Birkenhead suffragists had tapered off completely.

In November Lady Constance Lytton, on a speaking tour in the North West, came to stay with Alice who in turn attended her 'At Home' on 9 November 1909 in the Yamen Cafe in Bold Street. In January 1910, one day before Lady Constance was arrested disguised as the working class suffragette 'Jane Warton', she again stayed with Alice [4]. It is highly likely that the latter knew about Lady Constance's plans as on 14 February she noted laconically '"Miss Warton" arrested', thus indicating that she knew the name to be an alias.

Alice's diaries are not explicit as to why she changed her allegiance from the suffragists to suffragettes but they reveal certain tendencies. Throughout 1910 and 1911 she immersed herself in a range of apparently disparate activities. She campaigned for her friend, Miss Heaton, to be elected onto the Birkenhead Town Council. She continued to be active in the RSPCA, started to go to meetings of the Theosophical Society and became a member of the Hope Street Social Problem Circle in Liverpool (linked with the Unitarian Hope Street Church) to which she presented a paper on the Poor Law. Of all the Churches in Liverpool the non-conformist ones were most supportive of women's suffrage and Pembroke Chapel was a popular venue for major WSPU events. Alice had become part of a circle of radical non-conformist/Fabian socialist/women's suffrage supporters which spanned Liverpool and Birkenhead and included ministers as well as artists. Her growing involvement with the Theosophical Society seems to indicate that she was trying to link the political with the spiritual in her life.

For the WSPU she undertook a lot of hard, often menial work like selling the newspaper *Votes For Women* twice a week on train stations and on her own 'pitch', chalking pavements to announce meetings and events, minding the shop, accommodating visiting speakers in her home or speaking at the weekly open air meetings in Liverpool. She also enjoyed taking part in the more colourful WSPU events and trav-

elled to London for the monster procession in June 1911. Her diary entry: 'Up early, breakfast very punctually. A little before 9 went by (tram)car to Ferry and by 10 a.m. train from Lime Street to London. Meal at Eustace Miles Restaurant, then took place for procession. Wonderful meeting in Albert Hall. Train back to L'pool at 12.45, rather cold, and did not sleep much'.

Significant diary entries appear on 20 and 21 November 1911. 'Got things ready for going to London tomorrow, saw patients, got in stores. Wrote a good many letters and was anxious about expedition tomorrow'. Alice had volunteered to join the tenth Women's Parliament in London which would culminate in the usual ritual of small groups of women leaving Caxton Hall to seek access to the Prime Minister. This time the mood of the WSPU was particularly bitter because the Government's treatment of the so-called Conciliation Bill. It was hoped that this Bill would enfranchise women in 1912 and the WSPU had agreed to a truce on militancy while it was going through Parliament. In November it looked as if the Prime Minister was reneging on promises made around the

Bill's progress and Alice had good reasons to feel anxious about events on the day of the Women's Parliament. She wrote, in her usual sparse style: ' Went to London by 11 train from Lime St. Arr. 3.20, went to Lady Constance's flat, sewed for her, had a meal, went to Caxton Hall, walked about Parliament Sq., saw window breaking and arrests. Left Euston at 12 for home'. The truce had been broken and many women and even three men had been arrested and put in gaol. The law-abiding suffragists were furious as they didn't share the WSPU's mistrust of the Government and the events severely affected relationships between the major suffrage organisations nationally and locally. Having observed militancy at close quarters, Alice was not put off by it and in March 1912 she put her convictions to the test.

Militant
The point at which Alice Ker became militant was when the Government introduced a Reform Bill, which put the Conciliation Bill on which the movement had pinned so much hope on a backburner. Although the Prime Minister promised to allow a Women's Suffrage amendment to this Bill, the WSPU had had enough and declared war on the Government. Already besieged by massive industrial unrest and by the problems of Irish Home Rule, it was unable to handle the women sensibly. When Mrs. Pankhurst put out a call for a mass protest meeting on the 4th of March 1912, the police prepared for it but were taken by surprise by an unadvertised but highly orchestrated outbreak of window smashing on March 1st, graphically described by Sylvia Pankhurst: 'In Piccadilly, Regent Street, Oxford Street, Bond Street, Coventry Street and their neighbourhood, in Whitehall, Parliament Street, Trafalgar Square, Cockspur Street and the Strand (...) well-dressed women suddenly produced strong hammers from innocent-looking bags and parcels, and fell to smashing the shop windows. There is nothing like a hammer for smashing plate glass (...). Shop assistants rushed out; traffic was stopped. Policeman blew their whistles and called the public to aid them. Damage amounting to thousands of pounds was effected in a few moments. (...) Mrs. Pankhurst had meanwhile driven to Downing Street in a taxi and

broken some windows in the Prime Minister's residence. (...) Two hundred and nineteen women were arrested, but many window breakers escaped.'[5]

Despite public outrage a similar event occurred on Monday 4th, when Knightsbridge, Brompton Road and Kensington High Street came under attack. This time Dr. Ker, together with several other Birkenhead and Liverpool women were among the culprits! On 27 February she had caught the 9.20 train from Lime Street to London, seen off by her daughter Margaret. She went to stay with her sister Meta and spent the next few days calling on friends. On 1st March she wrote: 'Packed in morning and Meta dropped me from her taxi at Lady Constance Lytton, where I left my box. Then went to Clement's Inn and Women's Press and sold papers at Tottenham Ct Road. (...) Went with Lady Conny to Men's League meeting, splendid'. By then she knew about the first window smashing raid. On Saturday she was out again, selling *Votes For Women* in the street, pretty hazardous given the angry public reaction to the events. On Sunday '... Met others at Holland Pk at 6.50, and we went along to

Knightsbridge. Wrote letters before going to bed'. The following day she was arrested smashing windows at Harrod's Stores, Knightsbridge. At the Magistrates Court she was offered bail which she refused and was removed to Holloway Prison to await trial.

The Prison Letters
During this period she wrote a number of letters to her daughters Margaret and Mary, in which she explained some of her feelings about the WSPU and her reasons for being involved. After all, her deeds had been declared criminal and it was considered most shameful for a woman to end up in gaol. She had all reasons to expect serious repercussions for her social and professional status.

What follows is a selection of passages from her letters, which are otherwise devoted to reassuring and encouraging her daughters and telling them about life 'inside', and sorting out more practical problems, such as payment of rent, care for her regular patients etc..

5 S. Pankhurst, *The Suffragette Movement,* Virago reprint, 1977.
6 Self-denial week was introduced by the WSPU as a way to raise funds and also to remind members that the campaign required some sacrifice.

March 7th - whilst on remand

"... Go often to Renshaw St. (WSPU shop), I am sure that there will be much to hear. (...) From March 9. to 16. is a self-denial week [6]. Try to do without some things, and keep account of how much. You need not actually pay the money in just now, as you may be short, but keep the reckoning, and we will pay it into the War Chest later on. For instance, I think you might sell your theatre tickets for Saturday. I feel now as if I would never spend an unnecessary penny on anything else."

8th March

"I had a letter from Aunt Meta, forwarded from Somerset Ter. She is very sorry for the news in my letter, but says, very wisely, that there is no use discussing it. She also says she grieves over 'the check to our Parliamentary success' - poor deluded innocents! But still she wishes me well, and will be glad to hear when I am back to my 'deserted home' ".

9th March

"This morning I have a very nice letter from Miss Quirk. I can't answer her direct, but please thank her very much for it, and say she is not at all unworthy! As long as the great thing is near her heart she will soon find something that she can do for it and meanwhile, 'he that is not against us, is for us'. Give her my love. I am very glad every one is so nice to you, and I hope this may make many more understand the position."

March 11th - still not sure when she will have to appear in Court.

"...I am not allowing myself to think one way or the other how it is going to be, for it is quite impossible to tell. At the worst, we will all feel that we are making history and helping the Cause of right. (...). And I feel myself now a bar of tempered steel, not going to bend any more. After going through this, there is nothing more left in life to be afraid of. It is a very wonderful seasoning and perfecting. (...) There is a comical side to it all, too, I think that nothing better can be done with all the best workers of the nation than to shut them all up in idleness. It makes me think 'He that sitteth in the heavens shall laugh, the Lord shall have them in derision', I'm sure He does."

16th March

"A great many have gone out on bail, which is apparently being allowed at Bow Street (Magistrates Court). We poor Westminsters were not allowed it. Lady Conny tried for me and Mrs. Abraham for Dolly (her daughter, arrested at the same time as Alice - my note). Did you see the *Courier* of Wednesday, I think, with a description of us all? That ought to have been quoted to your man who called us Howling Dervishes. If he could only see the sedate old ladies who are in! (...) Make the most of all these evidences of respectability at any further debates or discussions. I believe the descriptions were put into the *Courier* to dispose of the hooligan cry. Some at the Artists' Club expressed great surprise that Miss Palethorpe should have been drawn into a Society which they understood, consisted chiefly of charwomen and persons of loose character! (...) When I come out, I think I am going to let the Nationals (NUWSS) know what I think of them, as well as the men. One sees clearly in this atmosphere, and, what makes even more difference, one has nothing left to be afraid of in speaking one's mind. Why should they not only not support us, the advance guard, as the rear guard should, but even fire into us from behind. No, I am associating with heroines here, and I don't feel inclined to suffer cowards so gladly as I have hitherto done."

March 18th - still on remand

"I am sorry Mrs. Abraham did not give me the chance of talking over the binding over with her (when she visited Alice in gaol - my note) but I am afraid it is not so common as you seem to think. (...) However, I will certainly take any chance consistent with honour, if I can do so without putting myself into the power of the police. I don't want to be run in if I speak at meetings, for instance. (...) Please write a p.c. (postcard) to Miss Willmer, 48 Wellington Rd, and tell her that my remarks referred not to her or her sister personally, but to their Society, the National Union. (...) Aunt Lisa brought me some newspapers. I see the miners are having a minimum wages bill rushed through for them - and yet people say that coercion does not lead to legislation. Mrs. Irvine's letter was all to that effect, feeling, she says 'that the whole action is a very grave mistake and that it greatly endangered the likelihood of the Conciliation Bill being passed and perhaps postponed for years the enfranchisement of women'. However, she does say, 'I am sure you think you are doing right'. I am afraid poor Cousin Susan had a great shock when she got my letter from Holloway, as she had not seen my name in the accounts. She says 'I do not approve of the methods of the WSPU as either right or efficacious. I believe you are very near the attainment of your aims & wish these methods were kept out of the campaign'. They cannot understand that but for 'these methods' we would be nowhere.

19th March

"Both Miss Dismore and Miss Wyse (members of Birkenhead WSS) sent me letters today, and neither of them says 'I am holier than thou'. I hear Miss Rathbone has been repudiating us again. I think even Miss Davies sees through her now; some others of us have done so for some time. I can't understand the National Union; they are really taking the Government's part against us. (...) I am sorry to have to be bound over, because of course the papers are saying that although the Suffragettes refused bail at first, they are all gladly agreeing to be bound over. But nobody will who can possibly stay here, and everybody agrees that I ought to go home if I can. Mind you, with part of me I am very sorry to do it, and if it were not that so many people need me, I would stay with the rest."

20th March

"Mrs. Pethick Lawrence was exercising with us today, and giving us such helpful talks. She has such wonderful spiritual insight, and this is a true spiritual movement, there is no doubt. I really don't think the National Union have at all the same deep feeling of the inward meaning of the whole movement; at least, I never felt it when I belonged to them. The vote is a mere symbol, but in fighting for it we are changing the whole outlook of womanhood all over the world. Aunt Ella is again moaning over the way in which our action has 'hurt the cause we all have at heart' ".

21st March

"I think I'll give my third letter to Aunt Ella today. She says 'pity us constitutionalists' for our actions; I shall say I pity them for everything, from their leader downwards! Did you see that Mrs. Fawcett was writing to Mr. Asquith offering the postponment of the Conciliation Bill? Such an unpolitical thing to do!"

23rd March - Margaret had sent her mother a telegram saying that she did not have to be bound over if she didn't want to - she and Mary would manage.

"... impress those National Union people with the way in which we of the WSPU feel that our struggle is raising us all up all along the line. Be very well behaved, both of you, and be as tidy as you can. Try to let Aunt Meta see that a Mother in prison influences you more than one out of it! You can really do as much for the Cause by making her thinking something of that sort as if you were going to prison yourself. (...) It is very interesting to watch the faces of our women in chapel, where we see most of them. Some are handsome, some pretty, some quite plain, but there is a peculiar Suffragette look on them all that transfigures each one. (...) The more I think about the National Union, the more amazed I am. No other political party repudiates its extreme wing. The Labour Party did not disassociate themselves from the rioters at Tonypandy, they just watched the case carefully to see that they were fairly dealt with, and nobody ever thought of making the moderate people responsible for the disorderly ones. That is why we say that they are so unpolitical, and that is why we are all here. If all the Suffrage Societies had stood firm, not necessarily approving, but not so elaborately firing into us from behind, the Government must have given way. As it is, they have simply played the Cabinet's game, which was to sow dissension and to break up the Suffrage ranks as much as possible. (...). I have your telegram which we all think splendid. Mrs. Pethick Lawrence strongly advises not being bound over. She says while you're in do the thing thoroughly while you are about it, and that is just my feeling. I hated the idea of going out and leaving the others. Now Miss Davies and I will probably stay together all through, as our charges are exactly the same. It takes all the sting out of punishment when you welcome it."

Dr. Ker was sentenced to three months imprisonment and was allowed to write and receive only one letter per fortnight. However she managed to have a few letters smuggled out. In one of these she mentioned a letter she had from the Secretary of the Birkenhead Rescue Home asking her to resign her position as Hon. Physician of the Home 'owing to a recent episode'. She felt very upset about this as she worked for the Rescue Home for several years. She decided not to resign - 'if they want to get rid of me, they must have the scandal of dismissing me. (...) I wonder how things will go with me, if the action of the Rescue Home will be followed by other people. I should think it is quite possible that I may find I have to leave Birkenhead, even if it were only to go over to Liverpool. I was prepared for this possibility before I left home, knowing that it might be the price I would have to pay".

It has often been said that it was much easier for middle class women actively to take part in the suffrage campaign, and risk arrest and imprisonment. This may be so, but for some, such as

Dr. Ker, a widow and parent, it was at considerable personal and economical cost. Her 'conversion' to militancy had been the logical next step when she realised that the struggle for the vote meant much more to her than gaining another right. For her it meant changing the world, for women as well as for men, and was not to be won without personal sacrifice. For her, being in the WSPU was as much a spiritual experience as practical action.

After her release from prison on 10 May 1912 she continued to work for the organisation. In August 1914 she moved to Liverpool where she took a house in the new Wavertree Garden Suburb development, became involved with war work (Welfare of Sailors' and Soldiers Wives) but remained active around women's suffrage. In 1916 Sylvia Pankhurst, in Liverpool to speak at a conference on women and sweated labour, stayed in her house.

In November 1916 Dr. Ker moved to London, where she spent the rest of a long and active life. She died in 1943, aged 90.

6

SUPPORTERS AND OPPONENTS

Notes
1 VFW, 3.11.1912.

So far attention has focused on the two main women's suffrage organisations in Liverpool, their membership, strategies and activities. It is important, however, to remember that although these were the driving force behind the campaign, Liverpool had several other groups, individuals and branches of national organisations who were supportive.

Other Women's Suffrage Societies

No mention has been made so far of other women's suffrage societies, although there were many which played a part in the campaign. The most significant of these was the Women's Freedom League. This organisation, of which Mrs. Charlotte Despard and Mrs. Theresa Billington Greig were founder members, did have several branches on Merseyside, but they were all shortlived and had only a small number of members.

The Tax Resistance League encouraged its members to withhold payment of tax as a protest against being kept without a voice in the running of the country. 'No taxation without representation' was the slogan. A member of the Waterloo branch of the Tax Resistance League had her goods taken in lieu of tax. When they came up for auction with a local auctioneer, Liverpool and Liscard suffragists held a protest meeting at which Patricia Woodlock gave a spirited address.[1]

The Churches

To enable their members to support the cause for women's suffrage within the framework of their religion, the churches in Britain set up national suffrage organisations of their own, often with local branches. In Liverpool a number of churchmen, Unitarian, Catholic, Baptist and Church of England were supportive and indeed active in the movement. They made church premises available for meetings and acted as chairmen or appeared as speakers at public events. In particular Pembroke Chapel, during the ministry of the Rev. Harry Youlden was the venue for many women's suffrage events.

The Catholic Women's Suffrage Society had a very active Liverpool branch with some 120 subscribing members. The Church League for Women's Suffrage established a Liverpool branch in 1912 and a year later counted 55 subscribing members. Several of these were also active members of the LWSS. Early on in its existence the branch experienced internal conflict over the acceptance of 'known militants' as members but managed to survive this. According to the Fourth Annual Report of 1913, Liverpool Church League had a branch banner but this is not known to have survived.

The Students

Liverpool University was co-educational from its very beginnings and women students did not have to fight for equal treatment by the institution in the same way as for example, their sisters in Manchester University. This didn't mean that they were not aware of the inequality experienced by women generally and in terms of citizenship in particular. In 1906 a Women Students' Suffrage Society was formed in Liverpool University. It flourished until the outbreak of war in 1914 which put a stop to much student activity. The Society organised debates and invited well-known national speakers on the subject. One of the students who was active from the start was Isabel Abraham. Her mother was a founder member of the Birkenhead and Wirral Women's Suffrage Society and mother

Catholic Women's Suffrage Society.

A Lantern Lecture

— ON —

"JOAN OF ARC,"

— BY —

Rev. T. J. Walshe.

CHAIR:

MISS ORMANDY.

—— AT ——

Hardman Hall, Hardman Street,

—— ON ——

MONDAY, FEB. 24th,

At 8 p.m.

ADMISSION 3d.
Reserved Seats, 6d. and 1/-.

Tickets may be obtained at the door, or by applying to the Hon. Sec., 66 Park Road South, Birkenhead.

Handbill by the Liverpool Catholic Women's Suffrage Society

2 The Suffragette,
1.11.1912, p.34.

Isabel Abraham, student

and daughter had both taken part in the demonstration in London in June 1908 mentioned above. Isabel was a member of the Council of the Liverpool Students Guild and active in a number of other societies.

A particularly interesting character was Margaret Ker, daughter of the Birkenhead G.P., Dr. Alice Ker. She became a student at Liverpool University in 1911. Margaret had been given a bursary of £30 a year from the Birkenhead Education Society. Margaret clearly shared her mother's suffrage convictions because on 28 October 1912 she was caught 'red handed' whilst attempting to set fire to a pillar box near James Street Station. She was taken to the nearest bridewell and charged with arson. In reply to this she stated, 'I did it as a Suffragette, I wish to point out that I did not do it for amusement, I had a reason.'[2] The phosphorus Margaret had used as an incendiary had done little damage to the contents of the letterbox and only a few letters had been partially charred but Margaret's right hand was badly burned.

After a week in gaol she appeared before the Stipendiary Magistrate in Liverpool. The plea from her lawyer that she should be dealt with leniently in view of her good character and the fact that she had already been punished by the damage to her hand was not accepted by the Magistrate. He committed her to the next session of the Assizes Court but agreed to bail in the meantime.

Three weeks after her arrest she

Margaret Ker leaving the court

tinguished attainments, imprisoned for the cause... and the daughter is following her mother in that activity on behalf of other women.'[3] He continued to describe Margaret as a bright scholarship student and pointed out that she had already been punished because of the injury to her hand. Sir Alfred Dale, Vice-Chancellor of Liverpool University, who had shown a great deal of sympathy throughout Margaret's ordeal, was also called to give evidence. His testimony about her character and success as a student was very positive but made little impact judging by the sentence she received - three months in the second division. However, thanks to his intervention Margaret was allowed back into the University after her release to complete her studies. She graduated two years later.[4]

The Men in the Movement
In Liverpool many men were sympathetic to the women's cause. These included local M.P.s, although most of them needed a good deal of persuasion to agree to take up the issue in the House. The most effective support, however, came from men who were politically active but did not hold office, such as

appeared in the Manchester Assizes. The trial was conducted in a court crowded with suffrage activists and was brief, but dramatic. Her defence made an excellent speech in which he pointed at Margaret's commitment to the movement, selling literature and taking part in demonstrations. 'She had seen her mother, a woman of culture and dis-

3 LDP&M, 23.11.1912, p.5.

4 A letter from Margaret to her aunt, describing her mother's arrest, is transcribed in Appendix 2, and letters from the vice president of the University to Margaret in Appendix 3.

radical churchmen, the more radical Liberals and a few Socialists. Some examples spring to mind.

Arthur Bulley was a prosperous Liverpool cottonbroker and devoted family man. He was, interestingly, also a Socialist and he actively supported women's suffrage. In 1910 he stood as Parliamentary Candidate for the Labour Party in Rossendale when he made women's suffrage one of the main planks of his campaign but lost, although perhaps not because of that. A year later he stood as Labour candidate for the Council elections in Liverpool. He had a passion for botany and gardening and went to live in West Kirby to create what is now known as Ness Gardens.

Walter Lyon Blease was a barrister and lecturer at Liverpool University and an active Liberal who lived in Croxteth Road. He wrote an influential pamphlet on women's emancipation *Against Prejudice,* published in 1910.

Most support came from the Liverpool branch of the Men's League for Women's Suffrage, established in 1908, which organised meetings especially for male audiences or sponsored open-air and other meetings organised by the women, both from LWSS and WSPU.

Arthur Allerton, an insurance agent living in Waterloo was a founder member and for several years the secretary of the League.

On Saturday 5 September 1908 the Liverpool Men's League organised a mass meeting on St. George's Plateau. The proceedings were organised around four platforms from which a range of speakers addressed the crowd. The majority of speakers were men and a very diverse collection they were: Mr. J.M. Mitchell, the national Honorary Secretary of the Men's League, Professor Alexander from Manchester University as well as Liverpool's Protestant Pastor George Wise, the Unitarian Rev. Mathieson Forson and the Rev. D. Roberts. The women speakers were Eleanor Rathbone, her niece the Manchester suffragist Margaret Ashton, Mrs. Swanwick, and several others. According to the *Liverpool Courier,* however, the 'star speaker' was Mrs. Nellie Martel, a suffragist from Australia with the reputation of being a very able and entertaining public speaker.

COPY OF LETTER TO

WOMEN'S SUFFRAGE CANDIDATE.

Liverpool Labour Representation Committee

Sec: ARTHUR W. SHORT.   Affiliated to the National Labour Party.

8, Brook Road, Bootle,
January 5th, 1910.

Dear Mr. BULLEY,

The above Committee learn with gratification that you are taking up the **Workers'** battle in **Rossendale**. We wish you every **success** and hope that **EVERY Trade Unionist** in the Constituency will give you their hearty support, knowing, as we do, how valuable an acquisition you would be to the cause we are working for, if **returned to Parliament.**

Yours faithfully, ARTHUR W. SHORT.

Mr. A. K. BULLEY.

WORKERS! FOLLOW THIS ADVICE

By voting for BULLEY

Printed and Published by C. Hargreaves, Burnley Road, Waterfoot.

5 Trades Council
Minutes, Liverpool
Record Office, TRA 331.

The Men's League continued to support the movement and worked with the LWSS as well as with the WSPU.

The Labour and Trade Union Movement

On the basis of the sources consulted for this study not much credit can be given to the Labour movement in Liverpool for supporting women's suffrage. This does not come as a surprise since the Liverpool trade unions were also slow to organise working women or welcome them into the Trades Council as representatives.

The Trades Council discussed women's suffrage for the first time in 1906, when John Morrissey, the husband of Alice Morrissey, moved a resolution. In this he asked for the Trades Council to express its condemnation of a sentence of six weeks imprisonment passed upon three London suffragists for a minor offence. This motion was passed with 34 votes to 12 but it is important to note the wording of the resolution, which was extremely cautious: 'That without expressing any opinion or otherwise of the agitation now being carried on for the attainment of the Parliamentary Vote for women, this council enters a strong protest against the unjust and cruel sentence ... etc.'[5] Mr. Morrissey must have known that a full-blown pro-women's suffrage motion would not have stood much chance. It is also important to note that the three London suffragettes in question were known to be working class women.

In January 1910 the Trades Council discussed, apparently at quite some length, 'the advisability of endorsing the candidature of Mr. A. Bulley for the Rossendale Division of Lancashire as a Woman Suffrage Candidate'. Luckily the vote went in favour of Mr. Bulley with a large majority.

Soon after, the Trades Council was asked to discuss two resolutions during the same meeting. The first one came from the People's Suffrage Society asking for support for a public demonstration on adult suffrage. The resolution was passed and the Trades Council agreed also to affiliate to the Society. A letter was then read out from the WSPU, written by Miss Flatman, asking the Trades Council to petition the Labour Party in the House of Commons to ballot for a Women's Suffrage Bill.

This request was rejected by 36 votes to 31, according to a report in the newspaper because such a Bill 'did not embrace manhood suffrage and was retrogressive'. This incident illustrates the divide within the fledgeling Labour Party nationally. The majority view was that to give women the vote on the same basis as men, i.e. those with a regular income, would favour middle and upper class women who were likely to vote Conservative at elections. It was the Labour Party's duty to campaign for voting rights for all adults, male or female, rich or poor. Later on, under the influence of Keir Hardie, the Labour Party changed tactics and for the time being supported votes for women on the same basis as men whilst aiming to achieve full adult suffrage on the long term.

In the same year the Trades Council was presented with a resolution from a Miss M.A. Hackey. She was one of the first female representatives on the Trades Council as member of the recently formed Dressmakers Union. The resolution read: 'That this meeting of the Liverpool Trades Council calls upon the Government to obey the will of the people as expressed by a majority of 109 of their elected representatives in the House of Commons, to provide the necessary facilities to enable the Woman Suffrage Bill to pass into law during the session'. It has not been possible to establish whether this resolution was actually passed. After 1910, no discussion of any importance took place in the Trades Council on the issue.

Little organised activity seems to have taken place amongst socialists in Liverpool around women's suffrage but a few individual members of the Independent Labour Party and the Fabian Society were quite involved, such as Councillor Morrissey and his wife Alice, already mentioned.

Staunch supporters were also **John Edwards**, the first chairman of the Liverpool Fabian Society and sometime editor of the Liverpool Labour Chronicle, and his wife. Both their names appear regularly in *Votes For Women*, either as financial supporters or as speakers. Although a committed Socialist, John Edwards was also an entrepreneur (iron founder), intellectual and Unitarian Christian and he and his wife moved in several different circles in Liverpool.

John Edwards

In 1916 John Edwards spoke at a rally on Equal Pay, at which Sylvia Pankhurst was the guest speaker. However, on several occasions he also took part in events organised by the LWSS.

The Artists

In Liverpool, as in other places, the movement received support from local artists. There was the National Women's Suffrage Artists League but there is no evidence of a Liverpool branch. However, the reports on events in Liverpool in *Votes for Women* makes regular reference to three artists in particular. They were all members of the Sandon Studios Society, a fashionable art society which counted many of Liverpool's intelligentsia amongst its members, including a number of known suffragettes.

Jessica Walker was born in Arizona and studied at the Liverpool School of Art. She had held a travelling scholarship and stayed in Paris and Florence. She exhibited on a number of occasions between 1904 and 1932. Apart from being a painter she was a critic and writer and correspondent for the journal *Studio.* She obviously was a supporter of women's suffrage as she was part of a

Liverpool WSPU election poster

delegation to the Prime Minister in June 1909; she was arrested and imprisoned. *Votes for Women* wrote that after a successful scholarship career she studied painting in Italy and Paris and was well known as a portrait and landscape painter. According to the same paper she designed the Liverpool campaign poster for the general election in December 1910. It seems that not a single copy of this poster has survived.

Miss Mary Cox Palethorpe was active in the movement from early onwards. She is mentioned as being present at the Annual Meeting of the LWSS in December 1900. She must have joined the WSPU after a branch was established in Liverpool and gave support by donating pictures for the offices and by decorating together with her artist friend, Miss Constance Copeman, the Sun Hall on important occasions. She assisted the painter David Jenkins with making the Liverpool banner for a procession in 1911. She was arrested taking part in a demonstration in London and imprisoned in Holloway Prison, at the same time as Dr. Ker.

David Jenkins was a landscape painter born in London in 1867. He had exhib-
ited at the Royal Academy and at the Liverpool Autumn Exhibition. From 1890 he had his studio in Pool Buildings, Castle Street and was a member of the Liverpool Sketching Club, the Liverpool Academy and the Sandon Studios Society. He, too, donated pictures to the WSPU offices and he designed the Liverpool WSPU banner. He lived in Birkenhead and for a while was the neighbour and friend of Dr. Alice Ker. He died suddenly in 1916 whilst doing war work in a local munitions factory. The Walker Art Gallery possesses two of his paintings.

The Anti-Women's Suffrage League
Serious concern about the impact of women getting the right to vote was quite widespread throughout the duration of the campaign. This concern had complex roots closely bound up with Victorian views about women's position in society. On the one hand women were considered to be too precious and innocent to become embroiled in public life, on the other hand they were thought to be too irrational and emotional to make an intelligent contribution. Whatever their abilities, their place was thought to be in the home. As

women they were also considered to be naturally conservative. The Liberal Party and later on the Labour Party feared the backlash of women's vote which they expected to be conservative. It was these general concerns which had kept women out of public life for such a long time. Those campaigning for women's suffrage were not helped by the fact that opposition to their cause included many women. In 1908 general concerns took on an organised form and a small group of well known women were instrumental in the establishment of the Women's National Anti-Suffrage League. The objects of this organisation were to resist the admission of women to the parliamentary franchise and to Parliament. Strangely enough it wanted to maintain women's representation on local councils and other bodies which were concerned with domestic and social affairs of the community. From December 1908, the League published its own journal *The Anti-Suffrage Review.*

In Liverpool an Anti-Suffrage meeting was reported as early as March 1908. It was held in Carlton Hall with leading 'Antis' as speakers. Apparently fourteen people joined the League and many more signed a petition. In October 1909 the *Liverpool Courier* published a letter signed by Miss Gertrude Currie from Liscard proposing the setting up of a Liverpool branch as 'the League now numbers many thousand members, and it is surely not right that Liverpool should be unrepresented'. In December 1909 a Liverpool branch is listed in the *Anti-Suffrage Review* with a Miss Owen of Warren Road, Blundellsands as secretary. She was succeeded in June 1910 by Miss C. Gostenhofer from Birkenhead who remained secretary until the organisation ceased to exist in 1918.

Not much is known about the make-up of the membership of the Liverpool branch. Men were admitted to membership and occasionally held positions on the executive committee. A Mr. J.C. Phillips, from Canning Street, was particularly active. In 1913 the *Anti-Women's Suffrage Review* gave a list of Vice-Presidents of the Liverpool branch, and these were certainly overwhelmingly Conservative in terms of party political allegiance. They were Lady Royden, wife of the Conservative

M.P. of Bootle, Mrs. F.E.Smith, wife of the Conservative M.P. for Walton, later Lord Birkenhead; Harold Smith, moving spirit behind the Working Men's Conservative Association; Colonel Chaloner, Conservative M.P. for Abercromby; Leslie Scott, Conservative M.P. for Exchange; Gershom Stewart, M.P.; Canon Paige Cox and J.S.Rankin, shipowner and later Conservative M.P. for East Toxteth.

The branch activities seem to have consisted of public and drawing room meetings, debating evenings with opponents and, in 1911, a mass canvass of local women municipal voters. The League's argument was that many more 'ordinary' women were against women's suffrage than in favour of it, and their canvass was an attempt to prove this. Cards were sent out to some 2000 local women asking them to place a cross for or against the Parliamentary vote for women. The League claimed that 75% had not replied; of those who replied two-fifths had been in favour of the vote and three-fifths against. The League held this result to be a clear 'anti' stance among ordinary Liverpool women but in doing so came up against the formidable Eleanor Rathbone. She,

through the LWSS, had conducted her own door-to-door canvass with a different outcome and criticised the League for its unprofessional methods.[6]

In November 1910 the League held a public debate with the puzzling title 'Women's social virtue was charity and men's courage'. The meeting was held at the WSPU office in Grange Road, Birkenhead with Dr. Alice Ker opposing Mr. J. Phillips. Apparently Dr. Ker was received with great enthusiasm and spoke about equal pay for equal work and how women had to fight to prevent things growing worse for women. On other occasions the League debated with members of the LWSS. Not surprisingly the *Anti-Suffrage Review* reports these meetings as a success for the League speakers, but reports in the local press do not always bear this out. On the whole it seems as if the Liverpool League was competently organised with up to ten local branches and a sizeable membership but mainly amongst Conservative Party supporters.

6 The Anti-Suffrage Review, February 1911, p.23; August 1911, p.160 and September 1911, p.184.

7

HOPES DASHED . . . BUT VICTORY AT LAST, 1912-1928

In 1912 and 1913 there were several moments during which it seemed as if Bills giving women a measure of voting rights were going to make it through Parliament. Unfortunately on every occasion other influences, including the attitude of the Prime Minister, Mr. Asquith, prevented this from happening. This raising and dashing of hopes had, not surprisingly, a serious effect on the suffrage organisations.

The NUWSS, despite a deep felt sense of disillusion, continued to campaign along the lines it had done, with one exception. In 1912 it decided to change its election policy. As we have seen, during elections the NUWSS used to support all candidates who as individuals supported women's suffrage whatever their political party. Now it decided to support the candidates who belonged to the only party which, as a *political party,* supported women's suffrage. This was the Labour Party. Thus, in cases where a Labour candidate stood against a Liberal candidate, the NUWSS encouraged its branches to support him. This change of policy was strongly opposed by Liverpool's Eleanor Rathbone, who was on the national executive committee of the NUWSS. An independent local councillor herself, she feared that it would involve the NUWSS in party political wrangles which could lead to splits. She tried to organise opposition against the policy within the NUWSS's Council but without success.

The effect of the Government's stubbornness on the WSPU was to reinforce its view that increased militancy was now the only road to success. Attacks on private property in particular were seen as an effective weapon, and acts ranging from the smashing of shop windows to burning down of property took place up and down the country.

In Liverpool both the LWSS and WSPU resumed their campaigning activities. Peaceful events such as a lantern lecture in Hope Hall ('The True History of the Militant Movement'), jumble sales, a fundraising whist drive and a performance of 'How the Vote was Won' kept the larger membership going but a smaller number inevitably expressed their disappointment in more militant ways. As we now know, with the benefit of hindsight, this not only made the Government more obstinate but also, sadly, lost the movement a good deal of public sympathy.

More Militancy

The eight day visit of King George V and Queen Mary to Lancashire and Liverpool in July 1913 was punctuated by expressions of suffrage militancy of perhaps a more eccentric and desperate kind.

On Saturday night, 5th July, a loud explosion took place in the neighbourhood of Liverpool Town Hall which was heard as far away as the Landing Stage. Investigations by the police showed that it was caused by a home-made device which had been placed in a subterranean passage of the Exchange Buildings, some fifty yards away from the Town Hall. The device had done little damage but the bang had attracted people from all directions and much speculation took place about the possible perpetrator. Although the suffragettes were suggested, no suffrage material confessing to the deed was left behind as was usually the case.

The next day when the King and Queen were due to arrive at Southport Promenade, a shelter on the Pier was set on fire and virtually burnt down. Because of the direction of the wind no further damage was done to the Pier but on a wall nearby a scrawl was found saying 'This good work deserves votes'.

More spectacular was the event on the following Tuesday, when the holiday retreat of the soap manufacturer, Sir William Lever, was set on fire. At that time Sir William and his wife were attending a house party given by Lord Derby at Knowsley Park in honour of the King and Queen. The summer house, close to Rivington Pike, was completely destroyed and with it a precious collection of paintings and tapestries. This time there was no doubt about the culprit as in the grounds of the villa a bag with suffragette literature was found and a message reading: 'If Sir William Lever had been as loyal to us and the Liberal Party as Lancashire is being to its King, this would not have happened.'

The next day a woman walked into a Liverpool police station and confessed to placing the home-made explosive on Exchange Flags and to the arson of Lord Lever's summer house. She was

Notes

1 P.Hesketh, My Aunt Edith,1966 Biography of Mrs. Rigby.

Mrs. Edith Rigby, wife of a well respected Preston medical man and a well-known suffragette. In a statement she made after having accepted the charges she stressed that she alone was responsible for what had happened and that she planned and executed it entirely on her own. As her reason she gave the consistent refusal of Government and politicians to take the women's claims seriously. The burning of Rivington Pike villa had been intended 'as a beacon lighted for the King and country to see that there are some insupportable grievances for women.'[1]

On the day the Royal Tour reached Liverpool the new secretary of the LWSPU, Miss Helen Jollie, caused a small stir. The procession was scheduled to pass South John Street where the WSPU had its offices at the time. Not only did the suffragettes knock in the windows of their own office, showering glass fragments over the onlookers who had gathered on the pavement below, but Helen Jollie came storming out of the building armed with a poker with which she smashed the window of a shop across the street. She was immediately arrested and taken into custody.

Elsewhere along the route another WSPU activist, Doris Callender, was arrested for having thrown a bouquet of flowers in the direction of the carriage; the bouquet had an envelope addressed to the King attached to it. This action must have been considered harmless as Doris was set free without charges being made against her.

These acts did much to turn what public sympathy with militancy there was into condemnation and ridicule. It should not be forgotten, though, that this apparently outrageous behaviour was a response to the Government stepping up its action with its force feeding of the hunger strikers, and passing of the so called 'Cat and Mouse Act'. Under this Act prisoners whose health was threatened by hunger strike and force feeding could be temporarily released and, once they had recovered from their ordeal, be re-imprisoned to serve the rest of their sentence.

The Pilgrimage
The NUWSS's last tour-de-force before the outbreak of the war was what became known as 'the Pilgrimage', a route-march from all corners of the country converging on London on the

26th of July 1913 for a mass demonstration in Hyde Park. The organisation involved in this monster event was impressive even by the most modern standards. Contingents of suffragists set out, on foot, from eight different starting points up and down the country and were joined on their way by fresh contingents. Thus Scottish women joined their sisters in Carlisle and Newcastle from where the two groups marched southwards along two different routes. The Carlisle group set out on 17th June and reached Liverpool on 5th July, having being joined by several hundred women on its way through the Lake District, Lancaster and Preston.

On their arrival at Colquitt Street the demonstrators marched through the main streets of Liverpool to the Exchange Flags for a meeting. They were headed by a brass band and displayed banners which showed that amongst those taking part were also the Conservative and Unionist Women's Franchise Association and the Catholic Women's Suffrage League. They carried mottoes emphasising the law-abiding character of their enterprise such as 'By Reason, Not By Force'. Councillor Eleanor Rathbone, Mrs. Nessie Steward Brown and Ciceley Leadly Brown addressed a largely sympathetic crowd, and according to the *Liverpool Daily Post* 'the Lady Mayoress and other ladies listened to a few of the speeches from the balcony of the rear of the Town Hall. Her ladyship seemed to be keenly interested and once or twice joined in the applause'.[2] It is interesting to note that on this occasion Keir Hardie, the first Labour M.P., also spoke. He described the enfranchisement of women as a human question upon which he believed the progress of the human race to depend. He told the men of Liverpool that 'not for the sake of their wives only but for their own sake and their children it was time that they had some new force in politics to act as a driving power towards sweeter and more humane conditions of life (hear, hear). The speechmaking concluded, the demonstrators, who numbered several hundred, fell into line, and headed by their band, marched down Water Street to the Landing Stage, en route for Chester'.[3] At the final meeting on 26th July in Hyde Park nineteen platforms were needed for speakers to be heard by the enormous crowd which had gathered to receive the marchers.

2 LDP&M, period 7.7.1913, p.9.
3 Ibid.

Liverpool suffragists taking part in the Pilgrimage. In the middle under the 'Law Abiding' banner, is Jane Colquitt.

The War and After

In 1914 the national women's suffrage societies had to decide what their response was to be to the outbreak of the war. Although bitter about the stubborn refusal of the Government to meet their demand, they nevertheless decided to call a truce, in order not to hinder the war effort. This meant an end to all action hostile to the Government for the duration of the war.

A number of leading members of the NUWSS were also pacifists who did not want to become involved with the war effort. However, under the direction of Mrs. Fawcett the NUWSS encouraged its 500 branches to undertake some sort of war work. At the same time it also decided that, despite the truce, the issue of women's right to vote must not be forgotten and that the organisation should be ready to resume an active campaign as soon as the war was over.

The WSPU's response was different. Mrs. Pankhurst, her daughter Christabel and other leaders took a heavily patriotic, anti-German stance and encouraged members to take a more aggressive part in the war effort.

They even became involved with recruitment for the army and munition works on behalf of the Government and would speak on platforms alongside the 'arch enemy', Lloyd George.

It is difficult to establish exactly what happened as a result of national policy decisions inside local branches on Merseyside. The publication of the WSPU's own paper, in 1913 renamed *The Suffragette* had been stopped after the truce and did not reappear until July 1915. It then had become devoted to anti-German propaganda and was rechristened *Britannia*. It ceased to give information about the movement locally.

The United Suffragists

It appears that in Liverpool the WSPU ceased to have an active local branch after 1914. Those women who wanted to keep in touch over women's suffrage and keep the issue alive during the war period had the opportunity to join the United Suffragists (US). This organisation had been formed after a leadership crisis within the National WSPU in 1914. A Liverpool and a Southport branch were reported to have been formed in March 1915.[4]

4 VFW, 19.3.1915.

The secretary of the Liverpool branch was a Miss Isabel Buxton, of 111 Queen's Road. The branch held its first meeting at Rushworth Hall. There appears to have been close links between this organisation and the local Women's Freedom League (WFL). On 12 May 1915 the branch organised a Florence Nightingale Commemoration with a procession to her memorial at the corner of Upper Parliament Street where a crown of laurels was laid. Thereafter a large and enthusiastic audience assembled at Pembroke Chapel on Pembroke Place for a joint meeting with the WFL at which Mrs. Despard was the main speaker.

In October 1915 the setting up of a Liverpool Women's Suffrage Club was discussed and invitations for two representatives sent to all known Suffrage Societies. The idea must have taken off as in November such a club opened with a Social Evening. A provisional club committee had been formed with a Mrs. Imlach as secretary. The United Suffragists obviously had an interest in wider issues concerning women as in 1916 it organised a meeting attended by about a thousand people (in spite of darkened streets) on the topic of 'Equal Pay for Equal Work'. Sylvia Pankhurst was the main speaker and gave many instances of sweated labour for women workers. On that occasion Mrs. Bamber (mother of Bessie Braddock), not known for taking any active part in the women's suffrage movement, also spoke. She appealed to women workers to organise themselves, criticising the male-dominated trade unions for their indifference. Mr. John Edwards spoke from the Socialist standpoint.

The report of the first annual meeting of the United Suffragists held on 28 March 1916 is interesting as it lists the newly elected officers of the committee. John Edwards was selected as president, Dr. Alice Ker as vice-president (conditionally) with Miss Buxton again as secretary. Given the fact that some of the ordinary members of the committee were also Fabians, one wonders whether the US had forged closer links with socialist/working class circles than previous local suffrage societies had been able to. In March 1917 at a meeting in the Clarion Cafe Dr. Ker withdrew as vice-president but was replaced by Annie Marks, one of the most active members of the early WSPU.

The Women Citizens' Association

It has not been possible to establish with certainty what happened during the war with the LWSS but there seems good reason to assume that a skeletal organisation continued to exist, due to Eleanor Rathbone's encouragement. It seems relevant to discuss here the establishment in 1913, of the Women Citizens' Association (WCA), entirely an initiative of Eleanor Rathbone. Set up as an educational 'wing' of the LWSS its aim was to prepare women for the actual use of the vote once they'd won it, which was not expected to take as long as it eventually did. The WCA became a training ground in politics for many Liverpool women who later in life were to play important roles in local civic life, such as Mabel Fletcher, (who became chair of the WCA in 1914), Jessie Beavan and the youthful Margaret Todd, later Lady Margaret Simey.

As it was established just before the outbreak of the war no Annual Report was published by the WCA until 1919. In this report a brief outline is given of the organisation's activities during the previous years. Apparently, immediately on the outbreak of war a joint meeting of the LWSS and the WCA was organised to consider how members of the Societies could best help the national emergency. Members were urged to offer their services to home front or medical organisations and it seems that thereafter members of both organisations became much involved with war work. Despite this the WCA made a determined effort to keep the Society going, regular meetings were held and members kept together so that, states the Report 'when in 1918 the Representation of the People Bill was passed, giving women over 30 the vote, there was an organised body in Liverpool ready to take its share in any new development of the women's movement'[5].

After the passing of the Bill there followed a period when the two organisations, the LWSS and the WCA considered their positions in relation to each other and in June 1919 it was agreed to amalgamate under the name Liverpool Women Citizens' Association (LWCA). The LWSS offices at 6 Lord Street became headquarters of the LWCA and Miss Parry was appointed Organising Secretary. By 1921 the LWCA had 12 branches organised on the basis of the electoral wards.

5 Liverpool Women's Citizens' Association, Report, 1919-1921, p.4.

A NEW FORM OF SUFFRAGE PROPAGANDA.

THE LIVERPOOL ASSOCIATION OF WOMEN CITIZENS.

Let me first describe the procedure of the Association of Women Citizens and then indicate the ideas which have led the Liverpool Society for Women's Suffrage to set it on foot.

The first step was to call a meeting of members of the Suffrage Society, to resolve to form an Association of Women Citizens, and to elect a small Provisional Committee, care being taken to include in this Committee women who were in sympathy with each of the three political parties.

The objects of the Association were defined as follows:—

1.—To foster the sense of Citizenship in Women.

2.—To encourage Self-education in Civic and Political Questions.

3.—To secure the return of Women Members of the City Council and Boards of Guardians.

4.—To secure, by law-abiding methods, the Parliamentary Enfranchisement of Women.

It was decided that the annual subscription should be sixpence, and that the organization of the Association should be by Wards, each being taken in succession and thoroughly canvassed.

The Association has already been set on foot in three Wards. The procedure, which it is intended to repeat at the rate of at least one Ward per month until the whole city has been covered, is as follows:—

1.—A Ward having been selected, a date about a month ahead is fixed for an Inaugural Meeting, at which the objects of the Association are to be explained and Members enrolled. A Chairman and two or three speakers are secured, and a Hall or Schoolroom in a central situation in the Ward is engaged.

2.—Cards of invitation for the Meeting are printed in two colours, one to be used for women voters and one for wives of voters. The invitation is issued in the names of the members of the Provisional Committee, and the Cards are addressed on the back, the names being taken from the register of voters. As the register does not, of course, show whether a

Victory at last

In 1917 it became clear that the Government, in anticipation of the end of the war and the return of so many young men from the front, would have to make arrangements for new electoral registers, i.e. lists of voters for each district. Wartime activities had made the old ones out of date. Only one in five of the eight million male voters still lived at their old address and many soldiers coming home after the war would be unable to vote in a General Election. It was suggested in Parliament that the old 'property qualification', the right to vote on the basis of income, should be dropped and that this right should be based on war service. The women suffragists were quick to point at the considerable contribution made to the war effort by women and it was obvious that the Government would no longer be able to exclude them from any new electoral arrangements it might want to make.

In June 1917 the House was presented with a Reform Bill, clause IV of which dealt with women's right to vote. This clause was disappointing in that it proposed to give the vote only to women householders, married women and women over 30, but it meant huge progress nonetheless! The Bill was passed by the House of Commons with a large majority and in December 1917 by the House of Lords. On 6 February 1918 the King gave the Royal Assent and eight and a half million women in Britain had won the vote!

In Liverpool the proceedings in the House of Commons had been followed with great interest and in February 1918 the *Daily Post* calculated that from the eleven newly created constituencies in Liverpool, 112,000 women could be placed on the electoral register. When in December 1918 a General Election took place, the LWCA presented the Parliamentary candidates in Liverpool with a list of questions submitted by affiliated women's associations. It publicised the responses of all the candidates and advised women electors to take note before they went to the ballot box. Although nationally the turn-out for the 1918 General Election was low compared to previous contests, women turned out in greater numbers than men, in some places in a proportion of three to one. In Liverpool it was thought that in some districts as many as 50% of women eligible to vote had done so. Not so, however, in West Derby where Sir F.E. Smith, Cabinet Minister and later Lord Birkenhead stood against a Labour candidate. Smith had been fiercely anti-women's suffrage whilst in Government and it is a matter of speculation whether this might explain the low turn out of women (25%) at the poll in that constituency. Whatever the case, it did not prevent him from winning the seat.

The campaign goes on!

As was to be expected, women in Britain were not going to be content with a democratic right unequal to that of men, who could vote at the age of 21. Ironically, in 1918 a Bill had also been passed allowing women to be Members of Parliament at the age of 21 and at subsequent elections women did stand for Parliament, albeit with little success.

The NUWSS, which in 1919 had changed its name to National Union of Societies for Equal Citizenship (NUSEC) was now under the presidency of Eleanor Rathbone and continued to agitate, together with many other national women's organisations. In 1928 the Conservative Parliament decided to extend the vote to all women over the age of 21 and introduced the 'Equal Franchise' Bill.

On 11 May 1928, when the Bill had been passed in the House of Commons and was about to be debated in the House of Lords, the LWCA called a public meeting. It was aimed at 'the younger women about to be enfranchised' and was chaired by Eleanor Rathbone. The two speakers were Miss Nancy Steward Parnell and Mrs. A.E. Edwards who, the *Daily Post* observed, were both under 30. They spoke on how women should use their vote in national and international affairs. Miss Parnell said that the vote was a big thing to be looked at in a big way. At the next election the whole country would be looking to its young women, and it would judge them by the seriousness with which they used their votes.

'We shall have to educate ourselves politically, and to choose our party ourselves. (...) But we must not be lost in any one party. We don't want to be like men. We want to make our own contribution to the welfare of the nation.'[6]

The debate in the House of Lords on the second reading of the Bill was reported by the *Daily Post*. There were still voices opposing the complete equalisation of women with men in terms of voting rights, but at least they did not vote against the Bill. Ironically it was Lord Birkenhead, for so many years one of the staunchest opponents of women's suffrage, who advised the peers to vote for the Bill, 'if without enthusiasm, yet in spirit of resolute resignation'.[7] They followed his advise and the Bill was passed with 114 to 35 votes in favour.

During the general election of 1929, Eleanor Rathbone stood successfully as an Independent candidate for Parliament. It seems wholly justified that she became Liverpool's first woman M.P.

6 LDP & M, 13.5.1928
7 LDP & M, 23.5.1928

2 J. 29

"DAILY POST"

Miss Eleanor Rathbone greeting Miss Nancy Stewart Parnell at the meeting in Liverpool, last night, for women who will be enfranchised under the Government bill. Left to right: Mrs. A. E. Edwards, Miss Parnell, Miss Margaret B. Todd, Miss Rathbone.

·8·

CONCLUSIONS

One of the aims of this study was to establish whether or not there was activity around women's suffrage in Liverpool and on Merseyside. This has been achieved to the extent that significant evidence, previously not available, has been brought together which points in the direction of a lively local women's suffrage 'scene' especially between 1906 and 1914. The study has been less successful, however, in establishing whether the movement in Liverpool developed along much the same lines as elsewhere and if not, how and why it was different. The almost complete absence of contemporary first hand testimony makes it difficult to draw conclusions from the secondary source material. This is particularly regrettable because Liverpool had such able and experienced leaders in the movement that an account of their personal experiences and views would have been invaluable. Given this situation, one can only suggest a few tentative conclusions.

The first stage of development of the movement in Liverpool, between 1870 and 1890, was very much an affair of a small circle of middle and upper class women and male supporters. In this, Liverpool differed little from London or Manchester. Special to Liverpool was perhaps the strong, almost exclusive connection with the Liberal Party. Undoubtedly some leading Conservative women had suffragist sympathies, but they kept a low public profile. An example of this group was Miss Harmood Banner, daughter of the Conservative M.P. for Everton whose contribution was to lend her drawing room for a meeting of women suffragists and to offer entertainment afterwards.[1] A branch of the Conservative and Unionist Women's Franchise Association existed in Liverpool which did participate in joint meetings with the LWSS. No evidence of it taking the initiative for public events has been found so far.

The election of Miss Eleanor Rathbone as secretary of the LWSS and her efficient and committed leadership gave a great boost to the organisation. Nevertheless, activities seem to have remained largely indoor and private until the establishment of a branch of the WSPU in Liverpool in 1906.

Previous to that a very small number of Liverpool women, such as Alice Morrissey, and perhaps Patricia Woodlock in her student days, had been connected with the Manchester or Lancashire branches of the WSPU. When the WSPU took off in Liverpool and the struggle for 'Votes for Women' was taken onto the streets, the LWSS must have felt pressure to change its tactics somewhat. This is evident during the election period of 1909-1910 when the LWSS hired shopfront premises and held open-air meetings and even a door to door canvass. At the same time the LWSS used the newspapers not only to advertise its activities but to criticise the militant tactics of the WSPU.

Throughout, there is a suggestion, although it is not stated explicitly, that the WSPU was an outside organisation after all and that the LWSS was the indigenous Liverpool organisation. It is difficult to characterise the LWSPU. There is no question about its liveliness and ability to attract a large number of women between 1908 and the outbreak of the war. The paid organisers, of whom there were three in succession, may all have been from outside

Liverpool but a significant number of Liverpool women were activated by them to the point of accepting arrest and imprisonment. The members sacrificed a great deal and a number of them took part in militant actions with almost spiritual abandon. There is evidence that several working class women were amongst them. However, the LWSPU did not survive the outbreak of the war and the change of policies of the National WSPU. Local members seem to have joined the United Suffragists instead or reverted to the LWSS or LWCA.

The impact of either the LWSS or LWSPU on local politics is difficult to assess. At the time of women's suffrage agitation the local political situation was very complex. It was dominated by the strife between Protestant and Catholic sections of the population and the manipulation of this by all the political parties. The party which in the early days of the suffrage movement had been so supportive, the Liberal Party, was losing ground in Liverpool after 1905 and suffered a crushing defeat in the national election of January 1910. Labour Party candidates might have been sympathetic to women's suffrage, but in Liverpool they were unable to win seats until much later and thus were of little use to the movement. In the circumstances it was very difficult for women to get the issue of women's voting rights onto the local political agenda.

It may well be that additional research will yield evidence which will sharpen the picture drawn so far. An examination of Walton Prison Records which may contain detailed prisoner's statements, or of records of the Liverpool Liberal Party possibly held at Headquarters still needs to be undertaken.

One of the more interesting and lasting results of the suffrage activity in Liverpool was the establishment by Eleanor Rathbone of the Liverpool Women Citizens' Association which eventually became a national organisation with the National Council for Equal Citizenship. Eleanor's understanding that it is not enough for women to win rights without practical political education in how to use them, is still valid today.

APPENDICES

Handwritten letter from the treasurer of the National WSPU to the Liverpool organiser about the establishment of the shop in 28 Berry Street. (Museum of London)

From Mrs. F.W. Pethick Lawrence
87, Clement's Inn
W.C.
July 28th, 1909

Dear Miss Flatman,

I have just received your letter. Why did you not tell me that you were going to get up this big meeting on Sep 13th. This fact certainly makes a difference to the case, I think you might be able to raise £50 in this meeting, and this as you say would go very far in paying a years rent and fitting and decorating.

I still think that just now on the eve of your departure to the Isle of Man and later for your holiday, it is unfortunate to enter into business arrangements which I think call for the close supervision of a responsible organiser. My experience of workmen is that they will always (.....) work and run up expenses if they are not watched. Everything that is done as an extra and is not definitely included in their estimate is charged at double or treble the rate of estimated work. Decorators make a habit of recouping themselves in a low estimate in this way. Haste and unconsidered detail is fatal to business. I am afraid you will meet with disappointment unless you are on the spot to supervise every detail. However, since you are so very keen about taking the shop, and since I have always found you reliable in business and money matters and since there is this special meeting coming on, I give my consent as Treasurer, albeit with a measure of reluctance, I must trust your judgement in this matter. As I say, I have confidence in your sense of responsibility and I should not put my judgement on one side in this matter, if I did not feel that you had shown evidence of your judgement. I cannot come to Liverpool, for we have overwhelming business just now at Headquarters. You have my sanction to go ahead with your scheme, I shall watch the result very carefully. In view of the hot (....) fight before us, I feel a deep responsibility in augmenting and husbanding the resources of the Union. I know that our staying power depends ultimately upon our finances. Good luck to you. I fully realise how you put all your head, brain and energy into the work that has been entrusted to you.

In haste.

Yours cordially,
Emmeline Pethick Lawrence

Miss Ada Flatman
28 Berry Street
Liverpool
April 22nd, 1910

*Typescript letter of
the Treasurer of the
National WSPU to the
Liverpool organiser
about moving into a
new shop at 11
Renshaw Street.
(Museum of London)*

Dear Miss Flatman,

I have been unable to answer your letter before owing to pressure of business.

If you think that to change the shop would be a wise move, by all means make the change. There does not seem to be any difference with regard to the business consideration as I think you already pay nearly £40 with rates and light for your present shop.

I am afraid there is not an opening in our new shop in London and I think it would be an immense mistake for you to change your work. You have just got hold of Liverpool, you have got your position there, the members are beginning to understand you and rally round you. You have made the campaign there a signal success. A great deal of this would be thrown away if you were now to change your sphere of work. For the year which ended on February 28th 1910, Liverpool takes the prize with regard to the financial side of the work. During the year, £465 was expended on the Liverpool campaign and £592 was raised. You started the present year with a balance of £120. This is a great feat of which you may justly be proud and it shows that you have established a very strong position in your local centre.

With all best wishes for great success.
Yours sincerely,

E. Pethick Lawrence

Letter from Margaret Ker to her aunt about her mother's arrest and imprisonment. Mrs Ker was eventually given three months, and was released because of ill health after she had completed two months. The letter is uncommonly informative about reactions from other people to suffragette action. (Family papers)

6, James Street
Thursday, March 7th, 1912
5.15 p.m.

My dear Aunt Meta,

Thank you very much for your letter, I'm sorry as I've had no time to answer it until now, but I've been tremendously busy both today and yesterday.

Mother was arrested on Monday at 10.30 a.m. She and Miss Davies, the Liverpool organiser & Mrs. Healiss broke some windows at Harrod's Stores, Knightsbridge, & they were all arrested together and taken first to Walton Street Police Station and then to Westminster P. Station, where they were all tried together on Monday afternoon. As their damage was more than £5 each they were committed for trial at the Quarter Session & remanded for eight days, i.e. until next Tuesday. The shopman who was giving evidence against them got into a muddle - at one moment he said that Mother hadn't done anything - then it came out quite plainly that she had, & she didn't deny it yet he couldn't unknit his first statement, so (Lady Constance Lytton says), they say she will probably get off. She was only one of the lot who was allowed bail, but she wouldn't take it as the others hadn't a chance of it. They were all sent to Holloway (in cabs, not in the Black Maria), & she will be there until Thursday, when her trial comes off. She is allowed to wear her own clothes & to get food in from outside, Lady Constance is supplying her with food, & I sent her a big basket of fruit this afternoon - it will probably be useful medicinally, as well as food. She is also allowed to write & receive letters. We got a letter from her yesterday, in which she says that her cell is quite airy & that everything is spotlessly clean. Both the sun & the moon shine in her cell window, but, as she points out, not both at once! She writes very cheerfully, & seems not at all downhearted.

Meanwhile Mary and I are getting on very well. Everybody is good to us. The people at school have said nothing at all to Mary about it. The people at College are very nice. Most of them think it a huge joke, except Miss Henderson, who, as you know, is rather older than the rest, but they are all nice, & sympathetically sorry for me (not at all pityingly or horribly), & none of them are disgusted or contemptuous. I am working very hard at College so that no one can say that Mother upset my work by going to prison. Mary is doing the same at school. Winifred and I are living a very seemly and peaceable life - we are quite model young women. After all nobody would say anything about Mother leaving us for pleasure, so why should they say anything about her leaving us for what both she & we conceive to be her duty? Mrs. Hillson across the road has just been over to say that we're to come to her for anything we want, & Mrs. Abraham, whose daughter is also in prison, says the same, & Lady Constance says we must let her know if there's anything at all that she can do for us. We are quite comfortable as far as money is concerned, because I have at last managed to get my £30 out of the Post Office Bank. Lady Constance and Mrs. Abraham had both offered to lend us whatever money we wanted, but of course this is much better. You see Mother had made all arrangements for us before she left home, & didn't leave us in the lurch. Of course I am using as little money as possible, & I have the bulk of it safely locked up. (.....)

Please don't be anxious about either Mary or me, because we're perfectly allright. I'll tell you if I hear any fresh news before Tuesday. Lady Constance is going to wire to me as soon as she knows Mother's sentence, & I'll let you know as soon as I hear.

I like your letter so much. Although I know you don't agree with us it was so dear & kind & non-controversial. Oh, I do wish you lived here, so that we could see you every day. It would be glorious.

Ever so much love to you from

Margaret.

From the beginning of Margaret Ker's trial, the Vice-Chancellor of Liverpool University, Dr. Alfred Dale, took a very supportive stance. In those days a student who was convicted would be asked to leave the University and the same treatment would undoubtedly have befallen Margaret had not the Vice-Chancellor intervened. There are a number of letters in his letterbook of 1912 concerning the case, several of which are to Margaret and her mother. It is clear from the letters that the Vice-Chancellor disapproved of militancy, but it is interesting to observe his mixed feelings about the particular case.

Letter to Margaret Ker, whilst she was waiting for her case to be transferred to Manchester Assizes. (Liverpool University Archives)

5th November 1912

Dear Miss Ker,

I must ask you to consider yourself as under suspension until the next meeting of the Senate, which will be held on November 20. What the decision of Senate will be is an open question; and until the last word has been said elsewhere, I am anxious that no discussion should arise here.

Believe me to remain, your very truly,

Alfred Dale, V.C.

9th November

Dear Dr. Ker,

Your letter does not (...) of the course that you propose to adopt. But if your daughter suffers as a result of this policy, I shall find it hard to forgive those who have advised her.

To me it is inconceivable that the sacrifice can 'redound to the advantage of the cause'. The indiscriminate destruction of letters is not an act that can be justified. And the methods of anarchy are strange proof of fitness for citizenship.

I hold, as I have done all along, that the thing done was not only foolish but wrong. Your daughter would not say no to that. But she is torn asunder by two loyalties that will not be conciliated and she will not condemn the act because she feels it would be to condemn the cause. She has my sympathy - but she does not carry my judgement in the slightest degree.

I am writing with incessant interruption, and cannot review or amend. Under other conditions I might have succeeded in putting what I have had to say in a less contentious form.

Believe me to remain, yours very truly,

Alfred Dale

Letter to Margaret's mother, Dr. Ker. She had informed Dr. Dale that the WSPU was to select its own lawyer for Margaret's defence. Mr G.J. Lynskey who had defended her in the Liverpool Police Court, had probably taken the case on request of Dr. Dale. This letter was hand-written and difficult to decipher.

Letter to Margaret Ker after she had been sentenced to three months imprisonment in the second division. In the intervening period the Vice-Chancellor had written her two more formal and short letters.

24th November 1912

My dear Margaret Ker,

Your letter came as a welcome surprise this morning for you have been much in my thoughts - and indeed in my heart.

I am more than glad that you have decided to act in the way that you describe; still more that you have decided not to do a thing that would have strained respect, if not affection, to the breaking point.

You will understand that my answer to your questions must be personal and not official. But as far as my knowledge of opinion in Senate goes, I should say that few, if any, would wish to send you down. Most, I believe, would be willing that you should return, take up your work again, and complete your course. They would require you no doubt to take no part in political agitation until your course was over. About Council, I am less certain; but I should hope that they would not press for a severer penalty than had satisfied Senate.

As to your continuance of your Studentship, I am less hopeful; but I do not despair even of that. The Birkenhead grant, I fear, has gone for good; that you probably assumed.

This is as much as I am able to say; but anything that I can do you may be sure will be done. Much depends on the result of your appeal to the Home Secretary; and until we know that, it is impossible to make definite plans. But it would not be wise in any case to come back to the University in the middle of a term.

I communicated the substance of your letter to your Mother early this morning; so she will not be anxious about you.

If things do not go as well as we hope, I shall try to come over and see you. Meanwhile, may I say this? You have shown that you are brave; now is the time you can be wise and patient too.

Believe me, affectionately yours,

Alfred Dale

2nd January 1913

Dear Dr. Ker,

Many thanks for your letter. I am sorry to hear that your daughter has been invalided; but a few days' rest and change will soon set her up again.

I hope that 'breakfast' does not mean a demonstration. It would be singularly unfortunate if, after urging the Home Secretary to let your daughter slip back into her place at the usual time, and with as little notice as possible, I should be called to account and asked to explain why she should begin with an act of this kind. But I cannot believe that this is what you have in mind.

Ever yours truly,

Alfred Dale

Margaret was to be discharged from prison on the 4th of January, 1913. The WSPU would treat her to the 'celebratory breakfast' given to all women on the morning of their coming through the prison gates.

Primary Sources

Constance Lytton Papers,
Joseph Edwards Papers,
Sandon Studios Minutebooks,
Women's Citizens' Association,
Liverpool Trades Council Minutes,
Liverpool Watchcommittee Minutes &
Annual Reports,
Liverpool Central Library Record Office.

Women's Suffrage Collection,
Fawcett Library, London

Women's Suffrage Collection,
London Museum

Women's Suffrage Collection,
Manchester Central Library Archives

Fabian Society Archives,
Library, Nuffield College, Oxford

Selina Cooper Papers,
Lancashire Record Office, Preston

Vice Chancellor's correspondence, *Liverpool
University Archives*

Dr. Alice Ker diaries, *private collection*

Women's Suffrage Press

The Anti Suffrage Review

The Church League for Women's Suffrage

Common Cause

Manchester National Society for Women's
Suffrage Journal

Suffragette

Votes for Women

Women's Franchise

Newspapers

Birkenhead News

Liverpool Courier

Liverpool Daily Post and Mercury

Liverpool Echo

Liverpool Labour Chronicle

Liverpool Porcupine

Labour Record

Southport Visiter

Weekly Mercury

Wallasey News

Books

The literature about the women's suffrage campaign is vast. The titles given here are a small selection of readily available books which have been useful for researching the Merseyside Story. A few autobiographies have been included.

Fulford, R., Votes for Women, *London 1957.*

Hesketh, P., My Aunt Edith, *1966*

Leneman, L., A Guid Cause. The Women's Suffrage Movement in Scotland, *Aberdeen, 1991.*

Lews, J., (ed.), Before the Vote was Won, Arguments for and Against Women's Suffrage 1864 - 1896, *London, 1987*

Liddington, J. and J. Norris, One Hand Tied Behind Us, *London 1978.*

Liddington, J., The Life and Times of a Respectable Rebel, Selina Cooper 1864-1946, *London, 1984.*

Lytton, C., Prisons and Prisoners, Some Personal Experiences, *London, 1914.*

Mitchell, H., The Hard Way Up, (1968), *London, 1977.*

Pankhurst, E., My Own Story, *London, 1914.*

Pankhurst, S., The Suffragette Movement, *(1931), Reprint London, 1978.*

Raeburn, A., The Militant Suffragettes, *London 1973.*

Raeburn, A., The Suffragette View, *London, 1976.*

Rosen, A., Rise Up, Women!, *London, 1974.*

Rover, C., Women's Suffrage and Party Politics in Britain 1866-1914, *London, 1967.*

Stocks, M., Eleanor Rathbone, A Biography, *London, 1949.*

Strachey, R., The Cause, A Short History of the Women's Movement in Great Britain, *(1928) London, 1978.*

Tickner, L., The Spectacle of Women, Imagery of the Suffrage Campaign 1907-14, *London, 1987.*

Waller, P.J., Democracy and Sectarianism, A Political and Social History of Liverpool 1868-1939, *Liverpool, 1981.*

LIST OF NAMES OF WOMEN WHO ACTIVELY PARTICIPATED IN THE WOMEN'S SUFFRAGE MOVEMENT ON MERSEYSIDE

This list is obviously not complete as it only contains the names of those women who made it into the press. Names found in the sources without any further information about address, or kind of activity undertaken, have also been omitted. Unless otherwise stated, the addresses are in Liverpool.

ABRAHAM, Mrs. C., 2 Kingsmead Road S., Birkenhead.
Initially involved with the Birkenhead and Wirral W.S.S. In 1906 spoke in defence of WSPU tactics at a meeting of the Wallasey Women's Liberal Association. From 1909 active for the WSPU; 1911 secretary of the Birkenhead branch. Also secretary of the Women's Local Government Association and the Women's Peace Society.

ABRAHAM, Miss Dorothy, 2 Kingsmead Road S., Birkenhead.
Took part in window smashing raid in London in March 1912. Refusing to pay a fine, she was sentenced to a month's imprisonment in Holloway.

ABRAHAM, Miss Isabel, probably Birkenhead.
Founder member of the Liverpool Student Women's Suffrage Organisation. Active in the LWSPU.

ASHBY, Mrs., 110 Liverpool Road, Birkdale.
Active member of Southport WSPU, as was her daughter.

AVERY, Mrs. Percy, 'Eldon House,' Victoria Road, Huyton.
One of the LWSPU's more affluent members. Involved from 1909. Chaired public meetings in Prescot, Birkenhead, the University and a mass demonstration on St George's Plateau. Regular seller of *Votes For Women,* her 'pitch' was at St James St. Station. Acted as secretary for *Votes For Women,* in 1911.

BARTON, E. Alice, 15 Upper Newington.
Volunteered at rally in Sun Hall to take part in delegation to Mr. Asquith in 1909. Arrested and given one month's imprisonment. Included in triumphal welcome home to released prisoners in May 1909.

BEAVAN, Jessie, 12 Ullet Road.
Sister of Margaret Beavan, Liverpool's first woman Lord Mayor. Member of the LWSS. Secretary of the West Lancashire, West Cheshire and North Wales Federation of Women's Suffrage Societies in 1911. Active member of the Women's Citizens Association and its secretary in 1926.

BIBBY, Miss Eileen,
Listed as member of the Manchester National Society for Women's Suffrage in 1870.

BINNS, Mrs. W., 'Oak Bank,' Oxton Road, Wallasey.
Wife of Rev. W. Binns. Member of National Society for Women's Suffrage in 1873. Husband present at public meeting in Hope Hall in 1873 where he proposed the resolution in favour of women's suffrage.

BOND, Miss.
Member of Wallasey WSS. Newspaper secretary for *Votes For Women.*

BOOTH, Mrs. A. (née Lydia Allan Butler), 46 Ullet Road.
Born in New York, Presbyterian background. In 1867 married the Liverpool shipping merchant Alfred Booth, Unitarian and Liberal. She was President of the Liverpool Ladies Union of Workers Among Women and Girls, possibly member of the Liverpool Fabian Society, President of the Victoria Settlement. Founder member and first President of the LWSS in 1894 and active in this organisation at least until 1914.

BOULNOIS, Mrs., Liverpool.
Member of the Committee of LWSS in 1895.

BOWRING, Mrs., and Miss, 'Terra Nova,' Sefton Park.
Both members of LWSS.

BRIGHT, Mrs. A. (née Edith Turner), 10 Mill Bank, West Derby.
Married to Allan Bright, general merchant and shipowner and leading member of the Liverpool Liberal Party. Mrs. Bright was honorary secretary of the Liverpool Ladies Union of Workers among Women & Girls. Member of the Freedom of Labour Defence Council, Secretary of the Liverpool Women's Legislative and Local Government Committee and co-secretary of the Diocesan Mothers' Union. Founder member of LWSS and its first Honorary Secretary in 1894. Active member, spoke at numerous meetings. She shared a platform at a public meeting with Esther Roper and Sarah Reddish, organisers of the Textile Workers Suffragists. Links with local socialists, spoke at Clarion meeting.

BROCKLEBANK, Mrs. Agnes, 'The Hollies,' Acrefield Road, Woolton.
Wife of Thomas Brocklebank, merchant and shipowner, director of the Liverpool and London Globe Insurance Co., Chairman of the South West Lancashire Liberal Association before 1885 and Liberal Unionist in 1886. Mrs. Brocklebank was on friendly terms with Mrs. Fawcett, president of the NUWSS. She was vice-president of the LWSS together with Mrs. Stewart Brown in 1894.

BROOK, Miss, later Mrs. John McGuchie.
From Huddersfield, she was part of the 1908 Lancashire campaign organised by Mary Gawthorpe. She was active in the WSPU in Southport. Spoke at many meetings. Imprisoned in 1912, presumably after window smashing raid in London.

BROUGHTON, Miss.
Part of the 1908 Lancashire campaign organised by Mary Gawthorpe. Involved in temperance work as secretary of the Southport Temperance branch. Secretary of the Pembroke Social Reform League and president of the Liverpool Women Workers Federation. Volunteered for the Asquith delegation during the rally at Sun Hall 1909 and was arrested and given a one month prison sentence in Holloway. Speaker at the protest meeting outside Walton Gaol after the imprisonment of suffragettes during the Haldane disturbances in 1909. After 1914 joined United Suffragettes.

BULLEY, Mrs. Raffles.
Sister in law of Arthur Bulley, Liverpool cotton-broker who stood as the women's suffrage candidate at the Rossendale by-election in 1910, Mrs. Bulley was a member of the National Union of Women Workers. She was involved with the Birkenhead and Wirral WSS from 1906.

BUTLER, Josephine, 348 Park Road, Liverpool.
Member of the Manchester National Society for Women's Suffrage in 1870. Initiated and almost single-handedly conducted the campaign against the Contagious Diseases Act. Very sympathetic towards women's suffrage but thought it unsuitable to be seen to be involved with both campaigns.

BUXTON, Miss Isabel, 111 Queens Road.
For several years secretary of the Liverpool branch of the United Suffragists but as yet little else known about her.

CALLENDER, Mrs. Doris.
First shopworker for the WSPU in 28 Berry Street. Imprisoned in 1912 after the window smashing raid in London in March 1912. Organised enactment of 'How the Vote was Won' in Wavertree Town Hall in June 1913.

CHUBB, Miss.
Member of the Liverpool Peace Society. Involved with LWSS from 1908, speaker at open air meetings and active during 1910 election campaign. On the executive committee of the Federation. Secretary of the Granby Ward branch of the WCA.

COLQUITT, Jane, 24 Teilo Street, Toxteth Park.
Became involved with LWSS, encouraged by Eleanor Rathbone.

COPEMAN, Constance, 2 Bridson Street
Studio at 5, Cook St.
Artist, member of Sandon Studios Society. Member of WSPU, contributed her artistic skills to the campaign.

COWLEY, Miss Emily.
Member of LWSPU. Arrested in London in 1908 after a Women's Parliament in Caxton Hall. Tried and bound over in Police Court. Must have been imprisoned as she received the Holloway brooch in 1909.

CRIDDLE, Helen, Liscard.
Involved in skirmishes with the police in London in 1907. No further details available.

DALBY, Miss H.H., Wirral.
Honorary treasurer of the Wirral WSS in 1909.

DEAKIN, Miss Evelyn, 9 Alexander Drive.
Active member Birkenhead and Wirral WSS and its branch secretary in 1912. On the executive committee of the Federation.

DISMORE, Miss, 65 Shrewsbury Road, Birkenhead.
Founder member of the Ladies Association of the RSPCA. Early member of the Birkenhead WSS, she remained a suffragist throughout her campaigning life.

DRYSDALE, Mrs. D.M.
Involved with the Women's Emigration Home in Colquit Street. Member of the first committee of the LWSS in 1895.

DUNN, Miss Edith, Claremont (also spelled Clare Mount), Wallasey.
'Captain' of the Wallasey/New Brighton district of the WSPU in 1909. On the Asquith delegation in 1909. Decorated the WSPU shop in 28 Berry Street and took part in the 'Pageant of Great Women' in Birkenhead in 1912.

EDWARDS, Mrs. John.
Secretary of the Liverpool branch of the Women's Industrial Council. Active Fabian and member of the ILP, and wife of the Socialist John Edwards. Seems to have become actively supportive of women's suffrage in 1912, when she is mentioned as having distributed posters over town for the LWSPU. Also supported LWSS events and chaired a meeting for the United Suffragists in 1913.

ELAM (or ELLAM), Miss Bertha, 48 Roscommon Street.
Ticket secretary for the second Sun Hall meeting in March 1909. Arrested on the Asquith Deputation in June 1909. Quoted in *Votes For Women* (1909, p. 877) that she '.... only began to live after she'd become involved with the WSPU.'

ESKRIGGE, Miss Edith, 23 Vale Drive.
Elected President of the Wallasey WSS at the 1911 Annual General Meeting. Paid organiser for the Federation, for whom she travelled the North West establishing a number of new branches for the NUWSS. Active member. Honorary Secretary of the WCA in 1926.

EVANS, Mrs.
Honorary secretary of the Women's Freedom League - Waterloo branch.

FORRES, Mrs, 'Mena House,' Birkdale.
Member of Southport WSPU.

FORSON, Mrs. Matthieson.
Member of the WSPU, open air speaker during 1908 Lancashire campaign. Most probably wife of the Rev. Matthieson Forson, a sympathiser of the movement and chairman for a number of women's suffrage meetings.

FORWOOD, Mrs. A.B.
Member of the first executive committee of the LWSS in 1894. Wife of the Conservative Mayor of Liverpool 1894. Her husband was Mayor of Liverpool 1878-90 and Conservative M.P. for Ormskirk 1885-1898.

FRIMSTON, Mrs., 8 Bertram Road, Sefton Park.
Member LWSPU. Organised recruitment meeting in 1912 during which several women offered to go on the next deputation in March 1912. Wife of Noel Frimston, cottonbroker, co-secretary of the Liverpool Men's League in 1910.

GAMBLE, Lady.
President of St Helen's WSS in 1909.

GRICE, Miss, 6 Ashfield Road, Aigburth.
Press secretary of the United Suffragists for a short period.

HALL, Mrs., Waterloo.
Member of the Waterloo branch of the Tax Resistance League. Her goods were confiscated and auctioned in 1911. Made her house available to census evaders in April 1911.

HARMOOD-BANNER, Miss, Askfield Hall, Neston.
Daughter of the Liverpool businessman, Conservative councillor and Conservative M.P. for Everton. She supported the suffragists by making her drawing room available for meetings.

HARRIS, Miss A.K., Devonshire Place, Birkenhead.
Member WSPU. Presided over open-air meeting at Birkenhead Park Gates and very active during the National Election campaign December 1909 - January 1910. Also in gaol in March 1912.

HEALISS, Georgina, probably 10 Church Road, Stanley.
One of five daughters of Frederick Healiss, boot and shoemaker. Joined the WSPU in 1906 but first mentioned as colour-bearer during Patricia Woodlock's triumphant home-coming after imprisonment in 1909. Arrested during the deputation to Asquith in June 1909, charged with wilful damage and imprisoned. Involved with the disturbances during the visit of cabinet minister Haldane to the Sun Hall after which she was arrested and imprisoned in Walton Gaol, where she took part in the hunger strike.

HEALISS, Mrs., 10 Church Road, Stanley.
Mother of Georgina. Initially supporting her daughter's activities, she herself became active. She was on the window-smashing raid in London in March 1912 and was imprisoned in Holloway. She was released early because of ill-health.

HEATHCOTE, Mrs., 21 Martins Lane, Liscard.
Member of LWSPU. Elected secretary of Wallasey section in 1911. Took part in 'Pageant of Great Women' in 1912.

HEPPEL, (or HEPPLE) Miss.
Member of LWSPU. Speaker at open air meetings in 1909. Seems to have been imprisoned at some point but no details found.

HETHERINGTON, Miss Amy, Fairfield.
Daughter of a solicitor. Having been interested in women's suffrage, she was recruited to the WSPU having heard Christabel Pankhurst speak in the Town Hall. She volunteered for the deputation to Asquith in June 1909 during which she was arrested. Like the other suffragettes from Liverpool she was given one month's imprisonment in Holloway.

HILLIER, Mrs.
Active as speaker during the WSPU Lancashire campaign in 1908. Was imprisoned, but no details found.

HILTON, Mrs.
During the rally with Mrs. Pankhurst in the Sun Hall, volunteered for the delegation of Asquith in March 1909. Had joined the WSPU after she'd heard Christabel Pankhurst speak only two weeks earlier. Was arrested in London and given one month's prison sentence.

HIRONS, Miss.
Captain of Great Crosby and Blundell Sands District WSPU, in 1909.

HOY, Miss, Highbury, Torrington Road, Liscard.
Member of the WSPU in Wallasey. Invited women to her home on the night of the census-avoidance. Took part in the 'Pageant of Great Women' in Birkenhead in 1912.

IMLACH, Mrs., 14 Canning Street.
Was secretary pro tem of the Liverpool Women's Suffrage Club, established in 1915.

JAPP, Olive, 24 Prince's Park Terrace.
Honorary treasurer of LWSS. Signed several 'Letters to the Editor' disassociating her organisation from militancy. Was on the Committee of the Liverpool Church League for Women's Suffrage in 1912 and 1913. Also on the Committee of the Federation.

JUMP, Mrs. T.
Active member of the Southport WSPU for which she chaired meeting and organised 'At Homes.'

KER, Dr. Alice, 'Skene House', 6 James Street.
Born in 1853, she was the thirteenth woman in Britain to get her name on the Medical Register. She became involved with the organised women's suffrage campaign from the beginning as founder member of the LWSS in 1894. However, she joined the WSPU when it was established on Merseyside. She defended militancy and took part in a window smashing raid in London, where she was arrested. She was imprisoned for two months in Holloway. She died in 1943.

KER, Margaret, 6 James Street, Birkenhead.
Born in 1892, daughter of Dr. Alice Ker. Whilst a student at Liverpool University she was caught in the act of setting fire to a pillar box. She was arrested and sentenced to three months in Walton Gaol from November 1912 to January 1913.

KERRIDGE, Miss.
Elected committee member of the Wallasey Branch of the WSPU in 1910. Took part in the Birkenhead staging of the 'Pageant of Great Women' in February 1912.

LEADLEY-BROWN, Cecily, Dawstone Hall, Heswall.
Involved with the LWSS at least from 1910. Addressed dinner hour meetings at factory gates of Port Sunlight and open air speaker during the 1910 election campaign. Correspondent to the *Common Cause* for the Federation. Active in the Liverpool Church League for which she spoke at meetings. Became involved with the Victoria Settlement in 1913.

LIPTON, Miss.
Member of the Birkenhead WSPU. Chalked the pavement during the Birkenhead campaign of 1909. Was also in charge of the shop funds.

LYSTER, Miss Geraldine.
Active member of LWSPU. Helped out with the shop and received a special mention for her activities during the 1910 election campaign in *Votes For Women*. Was charged at Liscard Petty Sessions in July 1910 with 'unlawfully defacing a Government pavement by writing on it,' presumably to advertise a WSPU meeting.

MACADAM, Elizabeth.
Co-worker and life-long companion of Eleanor Rathbone. Warden of the Victoria Settlement, Netherfield Road, from 1903. Active in the LWSS especially around the election campaign in 1910.

McGHEE, Miss.
Literature secretary of the Wallasey Section of *Votes For Women* in 1911. Took part in the 'Pageant of Great Women' in 1912.

McGUFFIE, Mrs.
Honorary treasurer of the Aintree branch of the Women's Freedom League.

McLAUGHLIN, Mrs., 6 North Brook Street.
Member of the LWSPU, she was appointed in 1909 as secretary of the Organisers Fund, to raise money for a paid organiser in Liverpool.

McPHERSON, Miss, 16 Newland Drive, Liscard.
She wrote to the Wallasey News in 1907 asking that a branch of the WSS be set up in Wallasey. Addressed dinner hour meetings at Port Sunlight, became secretary of the Liscard WSS and was elected to the Wirral WSS in 1911.

McTAGGART, Mrs, 'Ivy House,' Aigburth.
Honorary secretary of the Liverpool branch (short lived) of the Manchester Society for Women's Suffrage in 1872.

MAHOOD, Mrs.
Member of the Wallasey and Wirral WSS. Spoke at mass demonstration on St George's Plateau in 1910.

MARKS, Miss Annie.
Member of LWSPU since 1908 and reporter on Liverpool events to *Votes For Women*. Speaker during the WSPU Lancashire campaign in Liverpool. Spoke at open air meeting in 1909 before Mrs. Pankhurst's visit to the Sun Hall rally. Spoke at numerous open air meetings in Liverpool and the Wirral. Vice President (pro tem) of the Liverpool United Suffragists in 1917.

MEADE-KING, Miss.
Daughter of the Liberal councillor Meade-King, director of the Bank of Liverpool and philanthropist. She was a member of the first committee of the LWSS and an active member for years.

MILLER (MILLAR?), Miss Jessie, 15 Part Street, Southport.
Local exhibition secretary for the Southport WSPU in 1906. Volunteered for Asquith delegation in 1909.

MILLER, Mrs., 7 Liberty Buildings, School Lane.
Member of the United Suffragists. Financed a poster to be put up in Lime Street Station. Called a meeting in her studio in April 1915.

MORRIS, Mrs. Bessie, 2 Overton Street.
Member of the LWSPU from at least 1908. Presided over an 'At Home' in the Temperance Hall in Southport and subsequently in Liverpool when the Australian suffragist Mrs. Martel was touring the area as a visiting speaker in 1908. Volunteered for the delegation to Asquith during the rally in the Sun Hall in March 1909. Was arrested in London and gaoled. Spoke at many open air meetings.

MORRISSEY, Mrs. Alice, 305 Mill Street.
Wife of Liverpool's first Labour councillor, J.W.T. Morrissey. She was a Fabian and member of the ILP. Was a friend of Hannah Mitchell and other Manchester suffragists. Arrested after having caused a disturbance at a political rally at Belle Vue, Manchester. Imprisoned for two weeks in Strangeway prison, with Hannah Mitchell and Adela Pankhurst. Speaker at open air meetings and 'captain' of West Derby and Fairfield WSPU. Organiser pro tem in Liverpool in 1912. Died suddenly in November of that year.

MURPHY, Mrs. E.H.
Member of the WSPU. Speaker at WSPU open air meetings during the Lancashire campaign of 1908.

MYER, Mrs, (also spelled Meyer), 24(36) Oxford Street.
Speaker at a WSPU business meeting at 34 Oxford Street in 1908. Also at many meetings during the Lancashire campaign in 1908. Was on the delegation to Asquith in March 1909 during which she was arrested. She was imprisoned in Holloway. She was in charge of the sale of Votes For Women in the shop in Berry Street.

NOSWORTHY, Mrs. F.E.
Member of the Birkenhead committee of the National Society of Women's Suffrage, 1872.

NUGENT, Mrs. C.
Became involved with the WSPU almost by accident, whilst attending a demonstration outside Walton Gaol in 1910. Was arrested but released after intervention by her husband, a Liverpool magistrate.

O'BRIEN, Mrs., J.G., Fern Nook, Woodchurch Road.
Honorary secretary of the Birkenhead branch of the NUWSS in 1872. Also present at the 'women only' meeting at Hope Hall in 1880, where she seconded a resolution moved by Lydia Becker.

O'SULLIVAN, Miss, 6 Park Road, Southport.
Organiser of the WSPU 'At Home' in Southport in 1909, which she chaired.

OGDEN, Miss.
Member of the Wallasey WSS. Elected co-secretary at the AGM, September 1911.

PALETHORPE, Mary Cox, 14 Sandon Street.
Liverpool artist. Active in the campaign from
1900, eventually joined the WSPU. Donated
pictures for premises, decorated meeting halls
and contributed to the making of the WSPU
banner. Arrested during window smashing raid
in March 1912 and imprisoned in Holloway.

PARR, Mrs. Harry.
Member of the Southport WSPU. Organised
an 'At Home' at the Ladies' Club Room, Lord
Street. Recited at a meeting in 1910 in the
Cambridge Hall, with Mrs. Pankhurst present.

PARRY, Miss.
Was organising secretary of the WCA for several years. Resigned in 1920.

PHILIPS, Miss (or Mrs), Prince's Road.
Presided over the 'women only' meeting on
'Women and the Municipal Vote' in Hope Hall,
1880.

RATHBONE, Eleanor, Greenbank, Greenbank
Lane, Toxteth.
Born in 1872 into one of the leading shipping
merchant families of Liverpool. Her father,
William Rathbone, was an enlightened philanthropist under whose guidance she took her
first steps in the field of social reform. She
went to Oxford University and on her return to
Liverpool immersed herself in social work of
various kinds, as well as the women's suffrage
movement. She became Liverpool's first
woman councillor in 1909 and first woman
M.P. in 1929. In both cases she stood as an
Independent candidate. She is best known for
her campaign for family allowances which
ended successfully in 1945. She died in 1948.

RICHARDSON, Miss.
Member of the Wallasey WSS. Elected co-sec-
retary at the AGM, September 1911. (See
Ogden).

RIMMER, Mrs. E.J.
Daughter of a minister, she married a
Southport alderman. Mayoress of Southport.
Involved with local charitable work. Chaired
the first pro-suffrage meetings in Southport in
1888. Died in 1909.

ROBERTS, Miss Gladys.
Member of LWSPU. Mentioned as an 'ex-pris-
oner' in 1909, no details about this found.
Received the Holloway brooch from Mrs.
Pankhurst in the Albert Hall in 1909.

ROSLING, Mrs., 47 Sydney Street, Southport.
Member of the LWSPU. Local corresponding
secretary for Southport. Spoke at open air
meetings on the sands in Southport and in
New Brighton.

ROYDEN, Agnes Maude.
Born in 1876 into a prosperous ship building
family. Her father was a Conservative councillor in 1873, mayor in 1878 and Conservative
M.P. for West Toxteth 1885-92. Maude
became a preacher, very unusual for the time,
had socialist leanings and was an ardent suffragist. She was mainly active in London but
occasionally visited Merseyside as a speaker.

RUSSELL, Miss Jessie.
Initially with the NUWSS, later worked for the
Southport WSPU where she was an active
speaker at public meetings.

RYLEY, Miss Catherine (Kate), 46 Grosvenor Road, Southport.
Local philanthropist, social welfare worker, especially active in education for girls. She was a prominent Liberal and ardent worker for women's right to vote. Fiercely opposed to militancy.

SHAW, Mrs.
Honorary secretary of the Aintree Women's Freedom League, 1912.

SHERBROOKE, Mrs.
Secretary of the Southport Guild of the Unrepresented, 1888.

STEPHENSON, Miss C, 'Ashbourne,' Queens Drive, Walton.
Member of LWSPU. Exhibition officer for the National WSPU Grand Bazaar in 1909. Left in charge of open air meeting programme during Ada Flatman's visit to the Isle of Man in 1909. Organised Mrs. Pankhurst's visit and meeting in the Philharmonic in 1912.

STANBURY, Mrs.
Member of the LWSS. Active speaker during the campaign at the time of the Kirkdale by-election in 1907.

STEWART-BROWN, Mrs. Egerton, (née Nessie Muspratt), 16 Ullet Road.
Sister of Max Muspratt, first director of I.C.I., Liberal councillor 1903 and M.P. for Exchange in 1910. Mrs. Stewart-Brown had a wide range of social, political and philanthropic interests. She held leading positions in the Women's Liberal Association, the LWSS, the Women's Citizens Association and in later years the Women's Freedom League. She was founder member of the RSPCA. She was vice-president of the first committee of the LWSS in 1894 and remained active in it at least until 1914. She became a councillor, a J.P. and stood as Liberal candidate for the Waterloo Division.

TAYLOR, Mrs.
Member of the LWSPU. Attended Women's Parliament in Caxton Hall, London in 1908. Was arrested and sent to Holloway. Was on the reception committee for the next group of prisoners in May 1909. (Hosted an 'At Home' in Southport?).

THEW, Mrs., 27 Westcliffe Road, Birkdale.
Hosted a drawing room meeting of the Southport and District WSS in 1903. Eleanor Rathbone gave an address and nearly ninety people attended; spoke at Women's Co-op Guild, Churchtown. Presided over a meeting organised by the Southport Women's Liberal Association in 1908 at which Isabella Ford spoke on women's suffrage.

WALKER, Jessica (married name Stephens), 6 Brown Bldgs Exchange.
Born in Arizona, studied at Liverpool Art College. Painter, critic and writer. Actively supporting the WSPU, she suffered arrest and imprisonments.

WHITTLE, Mrs. Ewing, 1 Parliamentary Terrace, Liverpool.
Mrs. Whittle and her husband gave an 'At Home' in honour of Mrs. E. Cady Stanton and Miss Susan B. Anthony, the leading American suffragists of the day in December 1883. They were in Liverpool to undertake the return journey to the US.

WHITTAKER, Mrs. and Miss, 15 Holmfield, Park Street, Southport.
Miss Jannie Whittaker was elected exhibition treasurer for Southport in 1909 and organised the stalls for the London exhibition of the National WSPU. The family lent its motor car for an advertising cavalcade in 1909.

WILLMER, Miss J.A., Birkenhead.
Was on the demonstration organised by the NUWSS in London, June 1908. Elected vice-chairman of the Wirral WSS at the AGM in September 1911.

WOODLOCK, Patricia, 12 S. Hunter Street.
Daughter of the popular artist David Woodlock. Became involved with WSPU in Manchester (probably as a student) and the best known personality in the LWSPU. She was a coura-geous and tireless campaigner who spoke at numerous meetings. She was imprisoned five times, on the fourth occasion for a period of three months. The WSPU honoured her with the issue of a portrait postcard and *Votes For Women* devoted the front page of the Journal to her on the occasion of her release from prison in 1909. Was arrested in Birmingham when demonstrating at a rally with the Prime Minister and went on hunger strike when imprisoned. Information about her ceases after 1912.

WYSE, Miss A., 4 Mather Road, Claughton, Birkenhead.
Became honorary secretary of the Birkenhead WSS in 1900, held executive posts in the organisation on several occasions and was a regular speaker. Co-ordinated the Merseyside contingent for the great demonstration in London in 1908. Committee member of the Federation and later active in the WCA.